Napa Valley

NAPA VALLEY

Wine Tour

Artwork by

Sebastian Titus

Written by

Michael Topolos / Betty Dopson / Jeffrey Caldewey

Table of Contents

Foreword

TODAY IS PART OF YESTERDAY and foundation of tomorrow. The glory of Napa Valley wines in their own individual complexity was actually built by several generations of grape growers and vintners, men with pioneering spirits, hard efforts, personal sacrifices and beautiful dreams. Men of different cultures, different origins, they worked hard, step by step solving their daily problems with their own philosophy of "excelsior", upgrading their vineyards, selecting new methods of winemaking, wine aging and wine marketing.

The names of Jacob Schram, Charles Krug, Captain Gustave Niebaum, Georges de Latour, Jacob and Frederick Beringer, Charles Forni, Louis Martini, Elmer and Felix Salmina, Caesar Mondavi and so many others will live forever in Napa Valley history. Some of them, a long time ago, have left this beautiful valley, and some are still living and working together with their children and grandchildren.

As generations of men will come and go, the new generations of vineyards—the new plantings are replacing the old ones, and in centennial life of Napa vineyards, the law of continuous progress eliminates the obsolete varieties of grapes and the new selective vineyards, planted with aristocratic varietals such as Cabernet Sauvignon, Pinot Noir, Chardonnay and few others are opening new horizons for further success, further national and international victories.

Hand in hand with the experimental viticultural work done by University of California, the Napa Valley viticulturist of today pays far more attention to the general ecology, selecting for specific varieties new ecological regimes—new micro-climatic sub-regions of the valley, with proper soil and light exposures, assigning to the new vineyards better managerial techniques—such as formation of vines, pruning, nutritional security and rational qualitative productivity.

This influx to Napa Valley of the new generation of viticulturists is parallel with the new enological initiative of young enologists-winemakers, with their wisdom of conservative progress, granting new ideas and new techniques on the principle of accepting the inheritance of the past.

There is yet so much to do, so much to accomplish and I hope that in the future we never will stop working hard towards the new goals and further achievements, keeping our pioneering ideas not only as a privilege granted us from the past, but as our own duty for a better tomorrow!

Andre Tchelistcheff

Looking west across the valley from Howell Mt.

A Wine Valley Is Born

Napa County, with its fertile valley edged with dramatic hills, looks much like the Bordeaux section of France. It has a long and fascinating geologic history.

Its marine sediments were formed millions of years ago, in the Jurassic period and up to Miocene times, when the area was ocean bed. Sedimentary rocks exposed in Napa Valley during the transformation period are mostly sandstone, silts, limestones, cherts and conglomerates. Sandstone predominates; it is often mistakenly referred to by the wineries as limestone.

The valley was raised from the primordial sea, along with the rest of the continent. Slow yet tremendous pressures of the earth rising and folding caused sedimentary formations to bend and crack; volcanic action erupted, spewing extensively, burying earlier sedimentary crust under hundreds of feet of ash and lava. Molten glass poured from the earth, forming the obsidian outcroppings seen today on Glass Mountain, along Silverado Trail. These deposits were much valued by Indians for arrow tips and spear points.

These turbulences lasted for centuries, and gave a great variety of minerals. Aluvial deposits washed down from elevations, creating a fertile valley, covered with trees and lush vegetation where game abounded. It was crossd by creeks and rivers, teeming with fish.

Thus, through the happen-chance of Nature, a realm of unique beauty and utility to man was created. To its borders came migrations of Indian tribes, and the history of its human civilization began.

No story of the valley can be told without giving a prominent place to its Indian tribes. Although recent census figures show a present day Indian population of 215 persons, they lived here in thousands, in harmony with Nature, no less than 4000 years ago, as testified by the mummified body of an Indian girl, found in the Angwin area at the turn of the century. Arthur Atwood excavated the burial mound, which contained the body completely preserved in five layers of buckskin and pitch, "in a sitting position, knees tucked up with her arms around them." Carbon test determined the age of the body to be approximately 4000 years. Dr. Robert Heizer states in his "Anthropological Records" that a Glass Mountain excavation site implies occupation by Indian tribes at least 2000 years B. C.

The Indians were blessed with a life of beauty, simplicity and peace. They were natural conservationists, killing game as needed, drying the surplus for future use. They harvested acorns, berries and bulbs, to be eaten fresh and dried, realizing that some must be left to insure future crops. They wove beautiful baskets, lined with pitch for cooking.

These humble "digger" Indians were not inferior people of low intelligence, but survived in their society by knowledge and skills. They used a long digging stick to harvest their foods from the ground, hence the epithet "digger." The men hunted and fished, making camps

Looking west off Zinfandel Lane.

a short distance from spots where game was plentiful.

The sweathouse or temescal was the cultural center of each village. Here education, banquets, ceremonies and even hospitals brought the tribe together. Sweathouses were crudely-made oval structures of branches and mud, with a hole in the roof for smoke to escape.

The Wappos and Patwins comprised the largest groups of Indians. They had few cultural differences. The most evident of these was the ability of the more peaceful Patwins to ally themselves with the Mexican population, to the detriment of the neighboring Wappos. The Patwins had tribelets and settlements at Soscol, southeast Napa (Tulukai), and Napa (Termenukme). The Wappos were in Yountville (Kaimus), St. Helena (Annakatanoma) and the Hot Springs (Calistoga) area (Maiyakma, Niklektsonoma and Tselmenan).

Napa Valley Indians were clean, bathing daily, using the sweathouse and a fresh stream alternately. They had a high moral conscience, were religious, law abiding and aware of the importance of education. The young were taught the value of their cultural heritage, and a reverence for Nature. The name they gave this area was Ta-La-Ha-Lu-Si, translated "beautiful land," bespeaking their appreciation of esthetic values. Their most serious fault appears to have been their inability to adjust to the life styles of the white men who invaded this Eden.

The 10,000 to 12,000 Indians who lived here in 1831 dwindled during the next hundred years to a tenth of that number. Cholera epidemics and smallpox took most of their lives; many were lost during attacks by white men, who looked with indifference and contempt on them as beings of a lower order.

The Mexican revolt from Spain encouraged settlement to the North, and exploration and settlement of Napa Valley was part of this northward sweep. The Russian colony at Fort Ross posed a threat to the Mexican expansion, and Mexico, Russia and the USA vied with the Indians for possession of the area. The Mexicans, armed with their missions and militia, won out.

Mariano Vallejo had the resources to conquer, and in June 1823 the first expedition entered the valley. Mission San Rafael had been established six years earlier; another mission site was sought to the north. An armed escort led by Francisco Castro and Jose Sanchez left San Francisco and traveled to the areas of Petaluma, Napa, Sonoma and Suisun. Father Jose Altimira, after surveying these sites, chose to plant his mission cross in the Valley of the Moon, the twenty-first and final of the early Missions. Mission San Francisco Solano de Sonoma, 150 years later, is a familiar Sonoma landmark.

Although Napa Valley did not have a mission, it is indebted to Fr. Altamira for something quite different —a heritage of vines, olive and fig trees, and a golden trail of mustard.

It was the policy of the mission fathers that Indians should be rounded up, baptized and put to work for the Church. On the secular side, the Mexican government was giving out generous land grants to loyal citizens who would help to settle and expedite the expansion of their northern empire.

In the early 1830's, Napa Valley was a wild, adventurous land, attracting settlers from the east who had

The old Bale Mill north of St. Helena.

conquered one wilderness and sought another. George Calvert Yount came to the valley from South Carolina in 1831, becoming a hunter, trapper and friend of General Vallejo. His deeds of valor, as a pioneer, soldier and frontiersman, made him the most colorful American ever to ride into Napa Valley. He journeyed over the Indian trail to the top of Mount St. Helena, rising nearly 5000 feet at the head of the valley. Turning to look at the panorama below, with its ribbon of gold-blossoming mustard, he said, "In such a place I should love to clear the land and make my home; in such a place I should love to live and die." He fulfilled his vision, living there until his death in 1865.

The years between were eventful and exciting. He hunted sea otters along the coast. He visited the Petaluma adobe of General Vallejo as Indians were puddling clay for roof tiles, and told the General of his ability to make shingles. "What are they?" asked Vallejo. Yount took his axe and demonstrated the merits of redwood shingles, which pleased the General with their lightness and durability. Yount hired Charles Brown, recently arrived from the whaler "Helvetius," paying him $25 a month, plus room and board, for his services. Together they cut the trees, barking them, splitting them into eighteen inch blocks, then into shingles. Each could make about 1000 shingles a day. Vallejo was pleased when the job was finished, and offered Yount land in payment, since coin was scarce. Yount accepted readily, saying "Half a league will do."

The General's domain was vast, stretching to the Sierras. "We do not deal in half leagues here," he said. "You will take four leagues." "One league," Yount countered, for even this would require a score of Indians to manage and work it, and his sole capital was his axe. "Two leagues, nothing less," said the General in a firm voice. "You will take all of Caymus Ranch." So Yount became a Roman Catholic, baptized Jorge Concepcion Yount, and a Mexican citizen. Having fulfilled these requirements, the land grant was finalized, consisting of 11,814.52 acres in the heart of Napa Valley. His only neighbors were Indians. He built the first wooden structure in the county, a two-story Kentucky block house with portholes for protection against unfriendly Indians.

Yount understood and respected Indians; there was always a free exchange of information between them, to the betterment of both. Indians worked well for him, helping with improvements on his property. He planted vineyards, taking his grapes to Vallejo's winery; he raised sheep, horses and cattle, maintained fruit orchards, built a flour mill and a sawmill, and provided hospitality in the grand manner for all newcomers.

Yount's friendliness went ill requited. After the Land Act of 1851 threw titles of existing Mexican grant holders into confusion, squatters overran the valley. He claimed they caused him more trouble than Indians and grizzly bears combined. They took possession of his land, stole his cattle and fruit from his orchards, while he paid the taxes. Later, in 1855, the US government confirmed his Mexican title to the land.

After his death at 71 years of age, the name of the town, formerly called Sebastopol, was changed to Yountville in his honor. He can truly be called the father of Napa Valley.

Old La Perla Winery atop Spring Mountain.

The early 1840's found many immigrants arriving, farmers, not pioneers, interested in the plow rather than the axe. They could get land in three ways—perform services for it, buy it, or squat on it. They brought problems, challenged land grants, built fences. The land was very fertile, the wild oats growing above the back of a horse. It was studded with oaks, the habitat of elk, deer and bear.

Cattle were raised for food, but more importantly for hides and tallow. Large herds developed the first industry in the valley—tanning. The oak bark was taken from valley trees, and cured hides became a valuable export.

Equally as important were grapes. The Mission grape was planted on the ranches by the settlers; Indians trampled the grapes in a hide trough with bare feet, and the wine was fermented in skin bags.

Fenced farms began chopping up the land. The first major crop was wheat, reaped with a rough sickle, dried a day or two, and then horses were driven over it to thrash out the grain. Flour mills were erected, the remaining one being the Bale Mill, and sawmills were built for lumber taken from mountains and hillsides. Towns cropped up, and the Mexican Rancho period was ended; the era of agriculture began.

The 1840's marked an influx of covered wagon pioneers. History records that many members of the Bidwell-Bartelson party purchased land in the upper valley, as did settlers of the Grigsby-Ide party, between 1841 and 1845. Many of them returned East in a few years, claiming that all of the good land was gone and there was no opportunity.

Squabbles between contenders for the land, burnings, gunfights and Indian battles marked the beginning of the agricultural era. When the Gold Rush came, 49ers flooded the valley and left their impact on it. Gold fever sent many valley dwellers to the Motherlode to try their luck; many chose to return to their farms and extract their gold from successful miners wintering in the valley. Prices soared; the sale of two acres of onions brought $8000 to the farmer. William H. Nash, a horticulturist near Calistoga, sold his first peach crop, 100 peaches, for $100. Who needed a mine?

Development of vineyards on a commercial scale began in the late 1800's, after experimentation with wheat, barley and oats. Corn, potatoes, melons, pears, peaches, apples and grapes were grown on the ranchos, and oranges, olives, prunes and even tobacco were tried in this period.

The wealth of San Francisco at its feet and the success of vines in Sonoma County, augmented by the falling price of wheat, prompted the planting of the vine in Napa County. A table of profit in 1881 from two acres shows: Barley, $15.50; Wheat, $16.80; Corn, $27.25; Vines, $252.35.

The market for wine seemed unquenchable. Less fertile land in the valley, found to be unsuited to orchards and grains, proved valuable for vines. Men impressed with the valley came with wine on their minds, and set out to plant the available land. The state government aided them with research, publications, commissions and tax advantages. New vineyards were exempt from taxes for four years. Enthusiasm reigned.

Thanks to the colorful Count Agostin Haraszthy,

The old Occidental Winery built in 1878.

the European varieties were introduced about 1860. All but five of the 49 winemakers in 1879 were men of wealth, from European winemaking backgrounds. Prior to that time, wine made was of the Mission type. By 1867 there were 1000 acres in cultivation, with over 750,000 vines. The largest vineyard, owned by Sam Brannan, was 125,000 vines; the second was the Crane estate, with 62,000.

There was no stopping the flood tide; by 1881 there were 433 vineyards in the three districts of Napa, St. Helena and Calistoga, covering 11,043 acres. Ten years later there were 619 vineyards on more than 17,000 acres.

Early winemaking was primitive. The wine only satisfied local consumption; Idwal Jones reported of the Mission grape: "It was mediocre but useful, and the Franciscans wrought their honest best with it." But it was obvious that the future of valley wine did not lie there.

Charles Krug was the first to make non-Mexican wine in the county. In 1858, with his cider press and European wine knowhow, he proved a fine wine could be made from valley grapes.

Figures show the following rate of growth:

YEAR	GALLONS OF WINE
1860	8,520
1870	297,070
1880	2,460,000
1890	4,252,000

This increase brought on an overexpansion of vineyards and winemaking in the middle 1870's, and this, coupled with the Depression of 1874-77, sent many growers into bankruptcy. The industry was shocked, and began an effort toward planting improved European varieties, using new techniques of winemaking, which led to further expansion until the 1890 Depression sent the price of grapes to $8 a ton. This, coupled with phylloxera, knocked the growers to their knees, and gave the industry a blow from which it took years to recover.

Growers could not believe their vineyards were infected with the dread phylloxera, a disease without a remedy. It destroyed 10,000 acres; production fell from four million gallons in 1890 to two million in 1892, and to 407,612 gallons by the time it bottomed out in 1899.

The cure for the dread disease was found to consist of grafting to Vitis Riparia or Rupestus roots, and although financial losses had beggared many, the industry began to recover. New plainting were of superior varieties, and this created a sound basis for the agricultural community.

No sooner had the industry recovered than Prohibition came into the picture in 1919, with consequent closing of wineries and pulling out of vineyards. Many held on; no Italian, recalls an oldtimer, ever believed such an unnatural law could last. Until Repeal in 1933, a few wineries existed by making and selling sacramental wines; some shut down and let wineries fall into decline; vines were replaced by other crops. A few went on making and selling wine via the bootleg route, surviving by fair means or foul until the inexplicable madness was over.

Then came years of building back. A vineyard,

Los Carneros Vineyards below Milliken Peak.

like Rome, is not built in a day. Thus, instead of 200 years of solid, smooth advancement, the industry in Napa Valley can look back only about 40 years, a short time indeed in wine history compared with European centuries of developing and improving wines and vines.

In the history of the valley, a few names loom large. Among them are Jacob Schram, Gustave Niebaum, Jacob and Frederick Beringer, Charles Krug, Georges deLatour. These men came to the valley, some from affluence, some from poverty, with a dream so vast that to give their whole lives to its achievement seemed a privilege rather than a price to pay. They created a wine empire, built for the future, saw greatness ahead for valley wines. They lived as they made wine, with elegance and style, and their wineries have become valley shrines.

In the chronicles of the valley another people had an impact on the land—the Chinese. Almost none of them existed in the USA before 1850; then lured by visions of gold to be picked up in the streets they came to California, and remained to become the labor force behind the building of the wine empire.

They dug tunnels, made stone walls, toiled in orchards and vineyards, unhonored, unsung, little appreciated, often exploited. The 500 or so Chinese in Napa County left their mark on the valley; it can be seen today. The tunnels they dug, the walls they built, are humble monuments to a people who toiled long and hard, poorly paid, often treated with disrespect, yet always maintaining their own culture and self-respect. They are gone, but their influence lingers in the land they helped to build.

The history of the wine industry in Napa Valley has been a story of ups and downs, with very little time spent on middle ground. A legacy of growth and decline has culminated in the present building up on sound economic principles. Perhaps this has all contributed to character in the wine; if the industry had not suffered these series of traumas and triumphs, the wine might not be as good as it is today, for the best wine comes from the vine that must work harder to produce its grapes. To continue the analogy, it is doubtful if any valley winemaker today would admit to a life of luxury and ease.

Manicured vineyards along the West Slope.

Noble Vines & Vineyards

The story of wine begins in the vineyard. Vines are esthetically pleasing, and their abundance makes Napa Valley a refreshing sea of green in a dry California summer. On close scrutiny, each wine stands out and has its own personality, for grape varieties differ from one another and are individuals.

It is a fortunate fact that when vines go into an area, it inhibits housing tracts, and means that, for years ahead, the integrity of the land will be preserved, pleasing the senses and adding to man's well-being. Everyone recalls when Santa Clara Valley, a gloriously fertile area, was paved over—one of the finest pieces of agricultural land in the world was lost. With today's prospect of food shortage, this fact becomes alarming.

Here in Napa County, 25,000 acres are included in the Agricultural Preserve, created by an act of the County Board of Supervisors. Depending for its life on their action, it prevents the sale of land within its confines in small blocks, restricting it to tracts twenty acres in extent. The Preserve was enacted at a strategic moment in the life of the valley, in 1968, and has set a pattern for other areas wishing to keep urban encroachment at bay.

The life cycle of a vineyard is attuned to seasonal change, with each season bringing its own phase of plant life. After the harvest in August, September and October, the vine rests from its labors and gathers strength for another growing season. Growers always want sufficient cold to force dormancy in early winter, but this is rarely a problem in Napa Valley. Dormant vines are busy storing carbohydrates, getting ready, after hibernation, for a great thrust forward. Meanwhile the grower has time to work on his equipment and rest up for spring tasks; perhaps take a vacation.

In spring, the first warmth wakens the vine and starts its sap flowing. Its energies are high after a long rest, and it is ready to respond to pruning as weather permits workers to enter the vineyard. The pruning technique is one well-known method of quality control through limiting quantity. Before Pasteur's discovery of acetobacter, the effects of oxygen on wine, it was the most vital factor in wine production.

Pruning is always a hand operation, and the hand must be expert, for on the pruner's judgment hangs the quality of the crop. Cutting too heavily reduces potential tonnage. Insufficient pruning fails to insure proper bearing on the canes, involving the risk of overcropping, when the vine may produce more fruit than it can ripen. Competence here is vital to the vine's well-being and longevity.

Vines have a long life, from 90 to 100 years, and some vineyards in commercial bearing in Napa Valley are fifty and sixty years old. However, with the utmost in yield becoming daily more important, for reasons of economics, growers today plan to replant every 30 to 40 years.

When the ground is relatively dry, equipment is

Pritchard Hill Vineyards overlooking Lake Hennessey.

moved into the vineyard to turn under the cover crop. This puts nitrogen into the soil, and exposes the vine to maximum sunshine. It also gets rid of plants that compete with the vine for moisture and nutrients.

The greatest threat of spring is frost, which can cut potential tonnage drastically during the flowing season. Fortunes have been spent installing permanent-set irrigation systems, heaters and aeroplane engines to warm and circulate the air and prevent temperature drop below the critical 32 degrees.

Permanent-set irrigation requires large resources of water, which is not in plentiful supply here and often must be developed. But it is very effective in inhibiting frost damage. Water is sprayed on vines during frost periods and allowed to freeze; conversion into ice generates heat. A continual spray keeps water freezing and releasing its heat until frost danger is past. Severe winds and hail can also deplete potential tonnage by knocking flowers from vines before berry set.

Dusting is another important spring task; controlling fungus and organisms harmful to the development of the crop. Growth below the head must also be removed by suckering, to direct the vine's energy into balanced production. As the season advances, more spraying and cultivating may be necessary. It is vital for the vine to be able to photosynthesize enough sunshine to nurture and mature the crop.

Now the urgent chores are done, and the grower waits for the grapes to ripen. U. C. Davis designates a 214-day growing season, April 1 to October 31, for crop development. In Napa Valley, ripening of the crop is seldom a problem; what European grapes lack in sunshine is more than made up here. But in Europe, in a years with more than usual sunshine, there occurs one of those great vintages that produce noble wines, for grapes are able to develop more sugar, and thus more alcohol, body and character.

During the growing season, the grower must observe the grapes closely and test them frequently, for as sugar increases, acid decreases, and a most important factor in winemaking is proper sugar-acid balance.

The late summer ripening period is an extremely critical time, for now birds and deer begin to take their toll of the crop. Deer can jump a ten-foot fence to feast on the vines, and migrations of Starling populations from Oregon and Washington are monitored daily. These birds travel in flocks of thousands, and each bird can eat a pound of grapes per day. Vigilance on the part of the grower is at an all-season high during this pre-harvest period.

Fall brings the climax of the grape growing year; now weather is all-important, for untimely rain can lower sugar content by dilution, and can also produce mildew and mold. Workers move into the vineyards and the crop is picked diligently, for getting the grapes off the vine and to the crusher at the right time, and in good condition, is vital to making good wine.

Along with the cycle of seasons, there are other influences in the life of the vine: Soil, climate, grape variety and man.

Soil is basically an anchor for the vine, performing three functions: Depth sufficient for root penetration: Nutrients, and Water Retention Capability. With modern technology such as drip irrigation, soil depth is not

The valley's northernmost vineyard.

an all-important criterion in selecting a vineyard site. If soil lacks nutrients such as nitrogen, these can be provided with minimal problems.

Vines will grow in almost any soil; less well in heavy clay and in soils containing alkali salts. Heavy crops are produced on deep, fertile soil, but surprisingly enough, grape quality is better on soils of poorer fertility.

Vine roots penetrate the soil to a depth of about ten feet, and once a vineyard is established, it needs only about 20 inches of rain each year. Average rainfall in Napa Valley is 30 to 40 inches.

Soils vary from rich and deep to shallow and poor. Some vineyards are dry, and have no irrigation water, while others have drainage problems that must be corrected with drain tile systems. Most are non-irrigated, but water is always needed to get young vines established.

In some areas there are problems due to high winter and spring water table, which restricts root growth. Too much boron is a problem in some areas; dificiency of boron in others. Winter growth or cover crops supply some of the nitrogen needed for good production, and most vineyards do not receive additional fertilizers.

In Europe, food supply had to be considered before vines, with valleys left to grow grains and grapes planted on hillsides of necessity. This Italian and French influence came to California along with the wine grapes, bringing the idea that quality grapes must grow on hillsides to duplicate conditions under which fine wine is produced in Europe.

Many Napa Valley growers dry farm their vineyards and believe in the superiority of this method with an almost religious zeal, tending to frown on those who resort to irrigation to get bigger crops. Vineyards with sprinkler systems use them mainly for frost control, and to cool vines on days of extreme heat.

It is true that the more a vine must struggle to survive, the more character it will pick up along the way. It will be noted that the very fertile valleys of the San Joaquin produce bountiful crops of splendid-looking grapes, which, because of heat and fertility, are lacking in acid and character. This stems from a large skin-to-pulp ratio which tends to dilute flavor and odor constituents. Happily, soil and climate in Napa Valley are just the right combination to produce this desired character.

The climate of the valley, with its warm days and cool nights during the growing season, is recognized everywhere as growing incomparable grapes, with good sugar-acid balance and the character produced by just the right amount of stress. It is impossible to over-emphasize the impact of the micro-climate in this area; Keith Bowers, Napa County farm advisor, puts it this way: "Each grape has a micro-climate in the cluster."

Fitting grape variety to micro-climate is constantly being studied. With current grape prices, growers can afford to tear out old, spotty planting, replacing them with those exactly right for the location, and much of this has been done in the past few years.

Napa County lies in U. C. Davis-designated Zones I, II and III, but a more realistic division is into four major plant-climates, which may be classified as Maritime, Coastal, Transitional and Interior, depending on the degree of ocean influence.

West Slope seen from Larkmead Lane.

The Maritime area includes the section lying southwest of the city of Napa. Here the day vs. night temperature is a narrow range, as is seasonal change. Summer fog is characteristic of this section, known as Los Carneros, and it is best suited for early ripening grapes such as Pinot Noir and Chardonnay.

The Coastal zone extends from Napa to just north of St. Helena, and from the foothills on the east to the Sonoma County line on the west. As is typical of Napa Valley micro-climates, this can be subdivided into a cooler southern section, Napa to Yountville, and a warmer section north of the summer fog line of the Yountville hills. Going up the valley the climate gets warmer, for due to ocean influence, the south end of the county is, climatically, the north.

This Coastal zone is suited to growing both early and late maturing varietals of the finest quality, and is often called "Cabernet Country." The viticulturist-winemaster Andre Tchelistcheff says: "Cabernet needs Rutherford dust," and it is to this noble grape that most of the new plantings in this area are now devoted.

Beginning north of St. Helena at Lodi Lane on the south boundary, and extending to the town of Calistoga on the north, lies the Transitional zone, best suited to the later-maturing varieties.

The Pope, Berryessa and Chiles Valley areas are in the Interior zone, which is least influenced by cool ocean air and dominated by continental air. However, many other climatic influences bear on the micro-climate. Elevation and exposure of hillside vineyards in these valleys tend to influence interior valley heat toward coolness.

Rainfall varies in the different zones, with about 20 inches at Napa, 30 inches in the center of the valley, and up to 50 inches in the foothills. The temperature curve is another factor—if the temperature reaches 90 degrees in the daytime, it will be about 45 degrees at night, and this proportion, necessary for quality grape production, is almost constantly maintained.

The many small micro-climatic differences due to exposure, air, drainage and elevation each play a part in influencing the grapes. It can be said that everything in the environment influences the grapes.

There are now in Napa County 19,953 acres of bearing and non-bearing vineyard, with much of the planting done in the past eight to ten years. Great care has been taken to match grape variety to micro-climate, section by section, and much work and experimentation have been devoted to selecting superior stock. Isolating and propagating disease-resistant strains of varietal grape vines is a business of maximum proportions, and great stress is laid on locating and propagating clonal strains which have shown greater qualities of hardiness and plant vigor. Large scale methods of bench grafting and heat propagation of vines have been developed to insure a sufficient supply of young grape stock to meet the demand. All this is done to insure that, with proper handling, grapes will produce distinguished wines.

UC Davis has crossed varieties that grow best in this area to provide new hybrids that grow well and develop character in the state's big valleys, with considerable success. But it has been demonstrated that they can only approach, never equal, the noble varietals that Napa Valley grows superlatively well, such as Cabernet

East Slope vineyards near Calistoga.

Sauvignon, Pinot Noir, Chardonnay and White Riesling. Except for the native areas in Europe which developed them, these grapes are unsurpassed when grown in this small area of California.

The last great influence on the grapes is man himself—the man who plants, grows and cultivates the crop. Decisions made by the grower, month by month, year by year, have a profound effect on the vineyard. Vineyard management is anything the grower cares to make it, and his decisions make or mar the grapes on which quality of wine depends. This is no field for amateurs, but for skilled and dedicated technicians.

Man's influence on the land cannot be dealt with in depth without acknowledging our debt to the Indian, Chinese and Mexican laborers who helped build California's wine country. These people, of humble origin, had an affinity for the soil, and a commitment, inherent in their culture, to preserve and enhance the land, which those who come after them might well emulate.

The harvest is a very special event in wine country, the culmination of an entire year of effort. Picking grapes is a pleasure; the weather is warm, with fall in the air. The whole countryside turns out and works with a will, growers and their families bending to the task beside the hired pickers. It is a magical time, with the light-hearted gaiety of Christmas, and bringing a heightened awareness and quickened pace that sets it apart from the rest of the year.

Unlike any other crop, the life of a grape begins at harvest, and may go on for years, whereas other crops decline, and never become more and better than they are at harvest. With grapes, there is always a potential for something more. Each cluster picked will become a few sips of wine—perhaps great wine. This is an inspiring thought, and makes the labor of harvest light and big with hope.

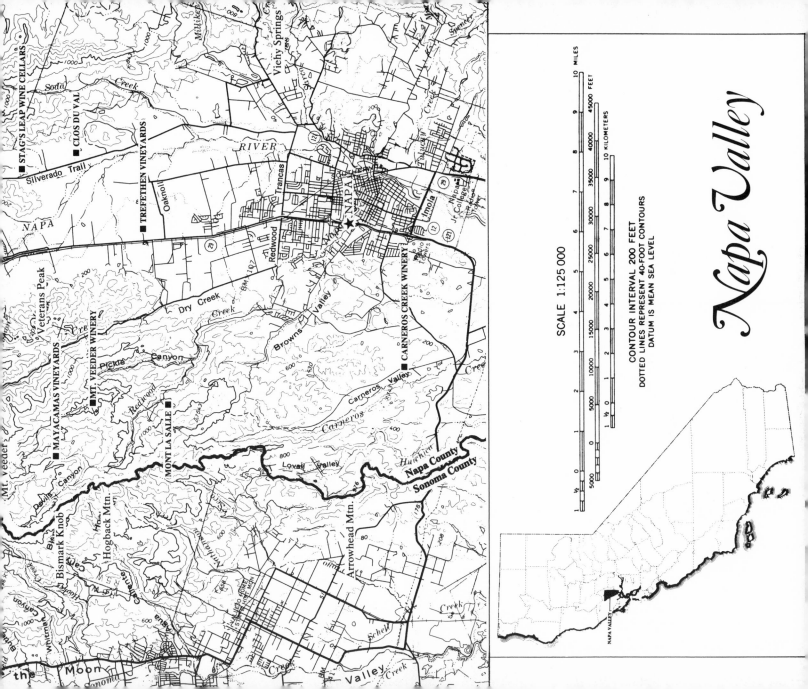

Napa Valley

SCALE 1:125 000

CONTOUR INTERVAL 200 FEET
DOTTED LINES REPRESENT 40-FOOT CONTOURS
DATUM IS MEAN SEA LEVEL

MILES
FEET
KILOMETERS

STAG'S LEAP WINE CELLARS
CLOS DU VAL
Silverado Trail
TREFETHEN VINEYARDS
Oaknoll
NAPA
RIVER
Vichy Springs
Trancas
NAPA
Redwood
CARNEROS CREEK WINERY
Imola
J Napa
College
Veterans Peak
MT. VEEDER WINERY
MAYACAMAS VINEYARDS
Pickle
Dry Creek
Creek
Browns
Valley
Canyon
Carneros
Valley
Carneros
MONT LA SALLE
Redwood
Bismark Knob
Hogback Mtn.
Devils Canyon
Lovall Valley
Huichica
Napa County
Sonoma County
Arrowhead Mtn.
Schell
Creek
the Moon
Valley
Creek

NAPA VALLEY

HE name Napa is a corruption of the Indian word "Nappa," as the natives at the mouth of the river called their settlement. When pioneer George Yount came here in 1831, he estimated there were between ten and twelve thousand Indians living in the Napa Valley. They lived peacefully but they possessed the universal trait of being unable to adapt to the ways of the invading white men. In 1833, cholera broke out and thousands of Indians died. Within a decade the Indian population of Napa Valley was decimated.

In 1845, a group of Californians, which later became known as "The Bear Flag Party," gathered in the nearby town of Sonoma to declare California's independence from Mexico. Two years later a member of this group, Nathan Coombs, surveyed the original town site of Napa. The city's first building was erected in 1848, but before its completion news of the discovery of gold reached owner Harrison Pierce causing him to abandon the project to try his luck in the gold fields. Pierce returned later that year disillusioned by his failure to find sudden riches and opened "The Empire Saloon."

Simpson Thomson planted the first European grape cuttings in 1852 on their Suscol land grant south of Napa city. Pioneer vintner Charles Krug produced the first European-style wine in the Napa region on the ranch of John Patchett in 1858. The wine industry of Napa Valley flourished partially as a result of Napa city's location on the navigational head of Napa River. Schooners plied her waters as early as 1841 and a steamship line to San Francisco was established in 1850, providing inexpensive and reliable transportation to the metropolitan market place. The valley opened like a cornucopia at the city of Napa which controlled the region's trade for almost a century.

With the advent of motor trucking systems, Napa lost its usefulness as the valley's market place. Commuting workers from nearby industrial centers have helped to quadruple the city's population since the end of World War II, precipitating the subsequent suburban sprawl. During the past ten years, growth in the guise of progress has devastated this one-time Victorian gem, and it has only been very recently that the local populace has made any attempt to rescue its history from the wrecker's ball.

A drive through the downtown residential section will reward the visitor with a glimpse of Napa's glorious past, with many fine examples of 19th Century architecture. Fuller Park, bounded by Oak and Jefferson streets, is a pleasant and tree-shaded siesta or picnic stop. The old Tolucay Cemetery on the east side of the river is the final resting place for many of Napa's citizens, both illustrious and notorious, including Mammy Pleasant, infamous madame and voodoo queen.

Two of Napa's famous ranches have been transformed into resorts. On the northern outskirts of town is the Silverado Country Club, originally the home of Civil War General John Miller and now a twelve-hundred acre resort complete with golf courses, tennis courts, five swimming pools, and 190 guest rooms. A drive out Coombsville Road (named after the city's founder) winds through a majestic valley and ends at Wild Horse Valley Ranch, a three-thousand acre estate offering Northern California's most comprehensive horse riding facilities.

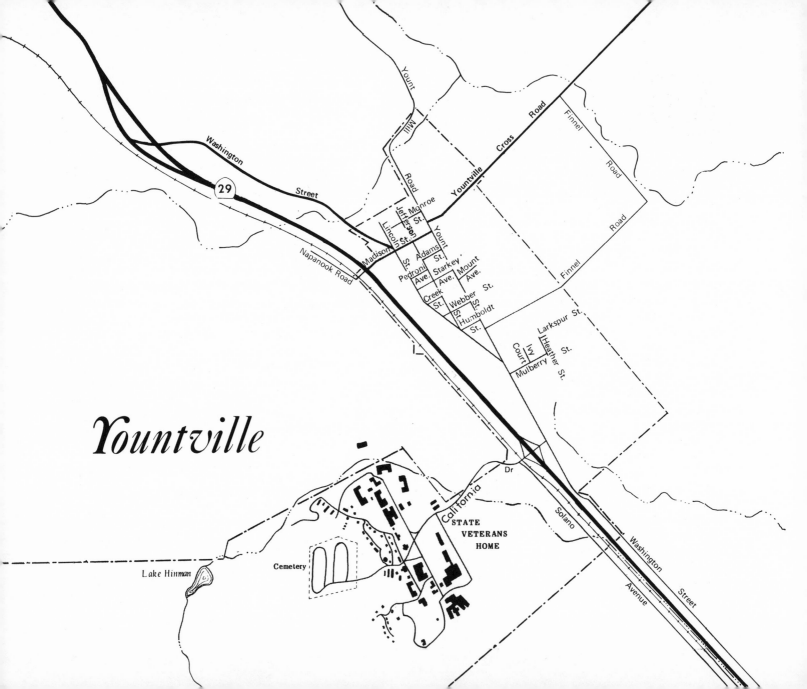

Yountville

THE first American to settle in the Napa Valley was George Yount, a representative pioneer - soldier - hunter - trapper - frontiersman, who came overland from North Carolina in 1831. Because he traveled the entire breadth of the continent, Yount was linked with many early events in the American occupation of the West.

Toward the end of 1833, Yount visited the Mexican missions in San Rafael and Sonoma and made the acquaintance of Mariano Guadalupe Vallejo, Commandante General of Alta California. Vallejo admired the ingenuity and resourcefulness of the intrepid pioneer and the two became lifelong friends. In 1835, Yount became a Mexican citizen and converted to Catholicism, baptized Jorge Concepcion Yount. As a reward for his loyalty and service, he was given a land grant consisting of 11,814 acres lying in the heart of Napa Valley. The "Caymus Land Grant" was the first in Napa county and Yount's dwelling was the area's first wooden structure.

Yount understood and respected Indians, at least to the extent that he was able to utilize their labor to his advantage without undue coersion. With their help, he planted vineyards, and took the grapes to Vallejo's winery. He also raised cattle and sheep, maintained fruit orchards, and built both a sawmill and a flour mill.

Rancho Caymus became a regular stopping place for immigrant parties. Yount greeted newcomers hospitably, let them camp near his home, gave them advice on where they could settle, and assisted them in exchanging their skilled workmanship for land. His friendliness, however, was ill-requited. After the Land Act of 1851 threw titles of existing Mexican land grant holders into confusion, squatters overran the valley. They took possession of Yount's land where they could and caused more trouble, according to Yount, than Indians and grizzly bears combined.

By 1855, a bustling village had grown on the southern border of Rancho Caymus consisting of two hotels, a blacksmith shop and two stores. After Yount's death at age 71 the town's name was changed from Sebastopol to Yountville in his honor.

George Yount's gravesite is in the cemetery at the corner of Jackson and Washington streets and is registered as a California State Historical Landmark. Part of the cemetery has, since its formation in 1848, been reserved for Indian burial grounds. Interred on this spot are the ashes of the local Wappo Indian tribes. On adjoining property is Yountville's city park, which provides convenient off-the-road picnic facilities.

A trip to Yountville is not complete without a visit to Vintage 1870. This two-story shopping complex was once the proud winemaking domain of Gottlieb Groezinger. Today quaint shops on the premises offer everything from gourmet foods and wine to crafts, clothing and antiques. The massive building houses a theatre where a performing arts group makes its home. One of the most spectacular sites here is the launching of a hot-air balloon manned by local aeronaut Steven Frattini. Reservations can be made for champagne flights aboard his multi-colored balloon, providing a truly heavenly view of Napa Valley.

DWARD BALE, an impoverished English surgeon, came to California aboard a whaling ship in 1834. He jumped ship in Monterey where he began medical practice. As surgeon to the Mexican forces, he met and later married General Vallejo's niece and subsequently became a naturalized Mexican citizen. In 1839, he was given title to the Carna Humana Rancho, a land grant that comprised all of northern Napa Valley, including what is now Calistoga and St. Helena. The entire property consisted of almost twenty thousand acres of virgin land.

In 1846, because of the demand for flour, Dr. Bale built a mill on a creekside location three miles north of the present site of St. Helena. Grist and flour were produced here for the next thirty years. The Old Bale Mill today has been completely restored and is a State of California Registered Historical Landmark.

In 1853, another Englishman, J. H. Still, purchased one hundred acres of property from the Bale estate and opened a general store. Two years later, Mr. Still, anxious to see a town started, offered to donate land to those who wanted to engage in business. By 1858, St. Helena was a flourishing town, complete with shoe shop, hotel, mercantile store, wagon shop, and, of course, the ubiquitous saloon. There is some dispute as to how the town actually received its name, but there seems little doubt the name was suggested by the fact that Mount St. Helena stands as a sentinel at the head of the Napa Valley.

Travelers journey north from the lower region of Napa to reach St. Helena at the very heart of the wine country. It is still a quaint Victorian village, little changed since the eighteen hundreds. Population has increased by scarcely a thousand souls in the last century, accounting for the pastoral quality of life in St. Helena.

St. Helena is the home of several institutions unique to the valley's winemaking industry. In the Ritchie Building, an ornate three-story architectural landmark built in 1896, are the studios of Vintage Image, publishers of this series of wine reference and guide books.

Several blocks away, off Adams Street is the Napa Valley Wine Library. Here is housed one of America's largest collections of wine-related books with rare and arcane volumes from all the enological regions of the world. Summer wine appreciation courses sponsored by the library offer an in-depth sensory evaluation experience.

On the outskirts of town, down Lodi Lane, visitors can see coopers assembling oak casks in the time-honored tradition. The Barrel Builders firm provides wood cooperage for many of California's vintners and also manufactures the inceasingly popular "hot tub" used for Japanese-style outdoor bathing.

St. Helena boasts two idyllic parks for picnickers. Crane Park, located at the end of Grayson Avenue behind the high school, is an isolated five-acre site with tennis courts, baseball fields, playground and restrooms. There are a dozen oak-shaded picnic tables complete with barbecues. Four miles north of town is Bothe-Napa Valley State Park. Dozens of picnic tables dot the 1242-acre park with hiking trails that wind off into the surrounding foothills.

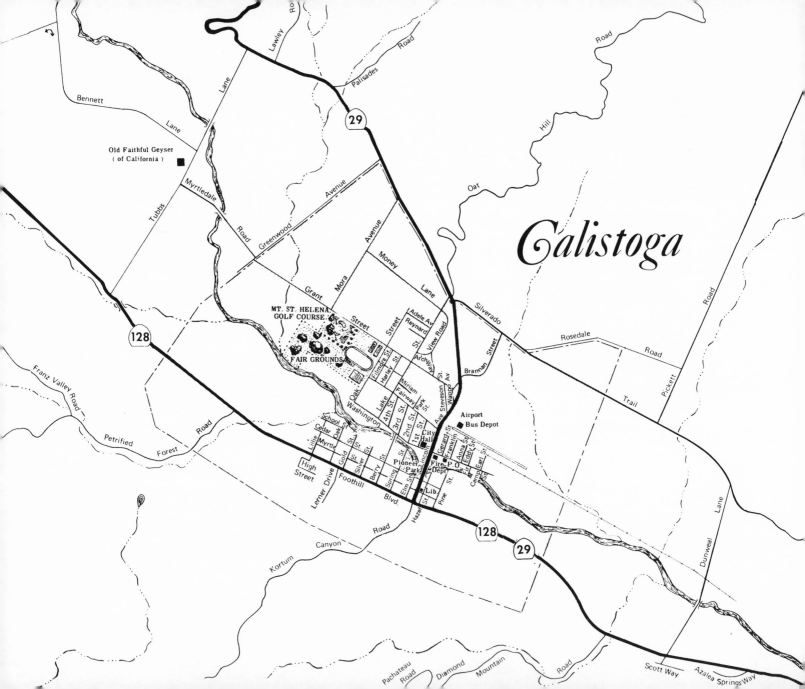

THE Indians were intuitively aware of the great medicinal value of Napa Valley's mineral springs. They wore trails through the densely wooded hills and valley floor making their regular pilgrimages to bathe in the health-giving waters. The first English speaking settlers here established a community which they called simply "Hot Springs," but the epithet "Calistoga" was coined by the near legendary California pioneer Sam Brannan.

Sam Brannan was twenty-seven years old in 1846 when he brought a shipload of Mormons from New York to Yerba Buena (now San Francisco). He subsequently established California's first newspaper and was the first to print word of the discovery of gold in 1848. During the gold rush, Brannan operated the only store in the entire Sacramento Valley. He subsequently became California's first banker, first land developer and first millionaire.

Beginning in 1859, Brannan acquired more than two-thousand acres at the foot of Mount St. Helena. It was his intention to establish the greatest resort spa in the West—a challenge which he pursued with great zeal, risking and eventually losing his entire fortune.

During 1860, the lavish main hotel and 25 guest cottages were built. The original general store at the corner of Wapoo Street is now dedicated with an historical marker. One of the guest cottages now stands across from the city hall and is scheduled for restoration by the Napa County Historical Society. The resort had an observatory where guests could get an aerial view of the entire countryside. It had many other special attractions: race track, golf course, swimming pool, mud and sulphur baths, skating rink, winery and distillery.

By 1872, Brannan had outspent his fortune. Hopelessly over-extended, he lost his interest in the resort and it was auctioned off piecemeal. Sam Brannan died penniless 20 years later.

Today there are six spas in Calistoga offering the same healthful hot mineral waters, steam and mud baths that made this area famous. Calistoga's Old Faithful Geyser, one of three such natural phenomena in the world, still erupts from the earth at periodic intervals. Some of the hoopla that attended Brannan's extravagent days in Calistoga returns each year at the Napa County Fair held the first week of July.

To Calistoga visitors, a breathtaking view of the whole Napa Valley is available from the cockpit of a glider. The engineless craft are towed aloft from the airport located on Lincoln Avenue to altitudes of several thousand feet. Tremendous updrafts created by the surrounding mountain ranges can keep the planes soaring for hours.

A similarly awesome view awaits the more earthbound traveler who takes the trip to Robert Lewis Stevenson Park atop Mount St. Helena. The famous author honeymooned here in 1880, and a plaque marks the spot where the newlyweds' cabin stood. A five-mile hiking trail leads from the park to the top of Mount St. Helena (elevation 4500 feet).

Pioneer Park, located in downtown Calistoga at the corner of Spring and Cedar Streets, offers visitors a quiet creekside picnic setting complete with redwood tables and barbecues.

Food

HE charming rural region of Napa Valley has a very provincial air which is in marked contrast to the cosmopolitan urban centers only an hour and a half away. It is sometimes assumed by sophisticated visitors that the only way to stave off starvation while touring the wine country is to pack a picnic lunch and then hurry home to dinner. There are, however, a surprising number of very good roadside bistros and eateries to be found secluded in this famous vineyard community. After all, the well-developed palates of the local populace cannot be sated by wine alone!

The intention of this guide is to help wine travelers looking for a good restaurant by providing them with a list of establishments which are in some way noteworthy.

A consensus of winery spokespeople and local restaurateurs initially compiled the list of restauarants selected for review. Restaurants have been carefully evaluated for freshness and quality of food, service, atmosphere and price range. No effort has been made to formally classify these restaurants; rather, the intent has been to inform the traveler of what to expect when visiting them.

For those interested in a picnic lunch among the vines, a listing of shops purveying provisions is included, as well as the wine shops which specialize in often hard-to-get local wines. Wine shop proprietors, not surprisingly, are often the most knowledgeable sources of newsworthy vineyard gossip and are usually more than willing to offer a well-informed opinion of the latest releases.

BON APPETIT   *Restaurant, Provisions*

An humble exterior belies the culinary expertise that awaits inside where loquacious Frenchman Richard Delisle and wife, Huguette, operate this country style cafe just north of Napa. Hugette learned her cooking talents at her Gallic mother's knee, while Richard is a former French enologist and wine consultant. They share kitchen responsibilities preparing house specilities fresh daily.

Bon Appetit serves lunches daily from 11:30 a.m. until 4 p.m. Customers can choose from quiche lorraine made with ham and bacon or quiche mariniere with shrimp and mushrooms. The homemade pates are available on the luncheon menu or by the slice for wine country picnics. The soups, which are prepared from scratch by Hugette Delisle, vary from hot French onion and cream of leek to chilled Gazpacho or festive Alsatian berry soup. Cheese boards, sandwiches and salads are also available. For dessert try their outstanding cheesecake or homemade chocolate mousse which, like other items on the menu, can also be purchased to "take out."

Wines from eighteen Napa Valley wineries are available by the bottle or may be consumed on the premises for $1.00-$1.50 corkage fee. The house wines are particularly impressive blends of varietal grapes made especially for Bon Appetit.

———

Bon Appetit, 4120 St. Helena Hwy., Napa 94558, Telephone (707) 252-7311. Hours: Monday-Saturday, 11:30 a.m.-5 p.m. Price range: $1.65-$3.85. Cards: BA, MC. Seating capacity: Inside 40, outside 25.

THE CARRIAGE HOUSE *Restaurant, Bar*

The Carriage House of the old Noye's family mansion has been transformed by its three enthusiastic young owners into a tasteful restaurant setting. The philosophy of Gloria and Bob Corbell and Edelle Vartan is exemplified by food imaginatively served and prepared fresh to order.

The lunches are modestly priced ($2.95-$3.25). The chicken-filled crepes seasoned with bechamel sauce come with a choice of very good homemade soup or zesty salad. During the summer season, tables are set up on the lawn for cafe lunches.

The dinner entrees are limited to six offerings with a daily special. Dinners include appetizer, soup du jour, salad, entree and coffee. Choices range from beef bourguignon in a red wine sauce with mushrooms and onions, served with potatoes and braised carrots, to the Friday special bouillabaisse, comprised of prawns, scallops and clams and fish in a spicy sauce, served with hot garlic bread.

The wine list offers selected wines from eighteen large and small Napa Valley wineries. Even a discriminating wine buff will be able to find a wine here to suit his palate.

———

The Carriage House, 1775 Clay St., Napa 94558, Telephone (707) 255-4744. Hours: Lunch, Monday-Friday, 11:30 a.m.-2:30 p.m.; dinner, Tuesday-Sunday, 5 p.m.-9 p.m. Price range: Lunch, $2.95-$3.25; Dinner, $5.95-$8.50. Cards: BA, MC, AE. Reservations suggested. Seating capacity 60. Full bar service.

CHICK'S HOUSE OF SPIRITS *Provisions, Wine*

While the wine selection at Chick's House of Spirits is not enormous, it is certainly the most comprehensive in Napa. Owners Chuck Cayhill and Mike Daley stock bottles from forty California wineries, including both large and small Napa vintners, attractively displayed in the large cellar room where a library of pertinent wine books is available for reference.

Adjoining Chick's is a delicatessen called "The Internationale" offering dozens of cheeses, meats, salads.

———

Chick's House of Spirits, 1220 Trancas, Napa 94558, Telephone (707) 224-0122. Hours: 9 a.m.-11 p.m. Monday-Thursday; 9 a.m.-10 p.m. Friday-Sunday. Cards: BA, MC.

THE DEPOT *Restaurant*

Originally owned by the Tamburelli family, The Depot Restaurant has been in operation for over half a century. The meals here are served Italian family-style with no frills, just immense quantities of food, first, a large plate of antipasto and French bread, followed by a big tureen of minestrone soup, and a salad. The pasta speciality here is Malfatti (light, spinach dumplings bathed in mild tomato sauce). The limited wine list includes recommended wines from Caymus Vineyard.

———

Depot Restaurant, 806 Fourth Street, Napa 94558, Telephone (707) 255-9944. Hours: Tuesday-Saturday 5:30 p.m.-10 p.m.; Sunday 2 p.m.-9 p.m. Price range: $4.25-$8.50. Corkage fee: $.50 per person. No cards. Reservations suggested. Seating 50.

JONESEY'S   *Restaurant, Bar*

The menu features steaks and salads. Steaks include top sirloin, sirloin club, filet mignon and New York and are served with a tossed green salad with Jonesy's famous blue cheese dressing, French bread and the house version of hash browns topped with cheese and onions.

People fly to Napa from all over Northern California to dine on steaks at Jonesy's. The salads here can be described in a word—huge ($1.50-$3.50). The tossed green salad with Romaine lettuce, green onions and blue cheese dressing, is topped with cottage cheese and an olive. The wine list features wines from nine of Napa Valley's largest wineries.

———

Jonesy's, Napa County Airport, Napa 94558, Telephone: (707) 224-2945. Hours: Tuesday-Saturday, 10 a.m.-9:30 p.m.; Sundays, 10 a.m.-9 p.m. Price range: $2.50-$8.25. Full bar. Cards: BA, MC, AE. Corkage $1.50. Reservations accepted. Seating 200.

OLIVER'S   *Restaurant, Bar*

The ambience at Olivers presents a semblance of elegance with gleaming crystal and silver, waiters in black tie and dimly lit bar. However, the cuisine does not quite live up to the decor.

Chef Candido Paz specializes in seafood dishes, most notably "Olivers creation" a combination of scampi provincale and fresh sole with a light champagne cream sauce.

———

Olivers, 1700 Second St., Napa 94558. Telephone (707) 252-4555. Hours: Dinner, 5:30 p.m.-10:30 p.m. Monday-Saturday; 5 p.m.-9 p.m. Sunday. Lunch: 11:30 a.m.-2:30 p.m. Monday-Friday. Price range: Lunch $2.50-$5.50, Dinner $8.50-$11.95. Corkage $2.00. Cards: BA, MC, AE. Seating 120.

PERRY'S   *Provisions, Delicatessen*

For visitors who might find themselves in downtown Napa wondering where to purchase picnic provisions, Perry's is the answer. The moderately-priced sandwiches ($.85-$2.00) are available with a variety of extras, including avocados. Lox, shrimp, raviolis, artichoke hearts and deviled eggs are all available, as well as baguettes of French bread and onion rolls. Homemade carrot cake and pecan pie are excellent desserts. The wine selection is unimaginative but an impressive stock of imported beers is kept chilled.

———

Perry's Delicatessen, 810 Randolph, Napa 94558, Telephone (707) 252-7044. Hours: 9 a.m.-10 p.m. Monday-Sunday. No cards.

RIVER HOUSE   *Restaurant, Bar*

The aptly-named River House rests at the bottom of a knoll on a tree-lined "Wind in the Willows" setting where a window table will assure you a view of the slowly moving river. The casual atmosphere created by the simple wood-panelled interior and flowered print tablecloths is contrasted by the half-dozen ruthlessly efficient waitresses scurrying about, never allowing an empty plate to sit more than a few seconds.

The Mario Bartolucci family's River House has acquired a reputation for its generous portions of prime rib au jus ($9.50), an enormous cut of carefully-aged beef available only on Friday and Saturday. It is served with an outstanding homemade soup, crisp green salad, baked potato and dessert, definitely not a meal for a light appetite. One example of their "Fish of the Day" is fresh filet of sole dipped in light egg batter and sauteed to tender perfection in herbed butter. The luncheon menu offers this dish served with an excellent clam-chocked chowder and French-fried potatoes for $2.95. Other seafood dishes on the menu include scampi, abalone and Australian lobster tail. The unexciting wine list offers bottles from seven large Napa Valley wineries.

River House, 505 Lincoln Ave., Napa 94558, Telephone (707) 255-9871. Hours: Lunch, Monday-Friday 11:30 a.m.-2.30 p.m.; dinner, Monday-Saturday 5:30 p.m.-10 p.m.; Sundays and holidays 5 p.m.-9 p.m. Price range: Lunch $1.75-$4.75, dinner $6.95-$11.95. Corkage $1.00. Cards: AE, BA, MC, DC. Full bar service. Seating capacity 100.

THE VICTORIAN HOUSE   *Restaurant*

The downhome Southern gentleman who greets you at the door is Nick Moorhead. He and his wife, Rose Mary, preside over this charming restaurant in an old Victorian house, faithfully restored to its original condition down to the furnishings and flowered carpet. The atmosphere is cheery and the service prompt.

Dinners include a home-made soup and fresh salad of lettuce, cucumbers and tomatoes in a light dressing. The Coq au Vin has been justly acclaimed and is at the same time the least expensive entree on the menu. Other entrees include shrimp curry, salmon au champagne, canard a l'orange, broiled halibut, lamb chops and steaks.

The Victorian House is perhaps best known for its Sunday Champagne Brunch. What a delightful way to start the day after a night of wine country revelry. The Eggs Victorian served en casserole on muffins with turkey slices, hollandaise sauce and a garnish of artichoke hearts, is the house specialty. Brunch comes with fresh fruit compote, blueberry muffins and a glass of palatable Santa Clara Valley champagne.

The wine list manages to feature wines from ten of the most well-known Napa Valley vineyards, most in full and half bottles. There is a one dollar corkage fee.

The Victorian House, 1778 Second Street, Napa 94558, Telephone (707) 252-4125. Dinner: Tuesday-Sunday, 6-10 p.m. Lunch: Tuesday-Friday, 11:30 a.m.-2 p.m. Brunch: Sunday, 10 a.m.-3 p.m. Price range: Dinner, $6.75-8.95; Lunch $1.95-$4.25; Brunch, $3.25-$4.25. Cards: AE, BA, MC. Seating capacity 42. Reservations suggested.

COURT OF THE TWO SISTERS   *Provisions*

This celebrated confectionary is owned and operated by two sisters, Hilda Auster-muehle and Leona Burns, with the able assistance of Hilda's brother and his wife. Starting as a hobby in their native St. Gallen, Switzerland, the pair have been involved in the creation of pastry all their lives.

The ladies moved to Napa Valley from Chicago after retiring for the third time. Now an offer to open a shop on San Francisco's Union Street has them packing again determined to divide their talents between the two operations.

Upon entering the shop, visitors are dazzled by the irresistable array of elaborately decorated confections. French pastries are created here with Leona modestly attibuting their success to the exclusive use of sweet butter. Napoleons, petits fours, truffles and tortes fill the glass cases, each one an individually designed work of art. The multi-layered "frog torte", decorated fancifully with dozens of cherubic frog's heads, has become a trademark of the Court of the Two Sisters. Quiche is made daily in both the Swiss and French styles ($3.75-$3.95).

The shop is located next door to the landmark Magnolia Hotel.

Court of the Two Sister, 6530 Yount St., Yountville 94599, Telephone (707) 944-2168. Hours: 10 a.m.-6 p.m. Tuesday-Sunday. No cards. Seating capacity: several small tables inside and outdoors. Coffee available on the premises.

THE DINER   *Restaurant*

Many locals consider The Diner in Yountville to be the only place in the Napa Valley to eat breakfast, and with good reason. The menu ranges from traditional bacon and eggs to avocado and sour cream omelettes to Mexican omelettes with cheese, olives, tomatoes and chile sauce, all generously served with grilled potatoes and toasted sourdough French bread.

A backyard garden provides the freshest possible vegetables; pies and cakes are homemade; orders are prepared individually and served with friendly, prompt efficiency.

The lunch menu features a dozen different hot and cold sandwiches and such specialities as the Humdinger —a cheeseburger on a grilled English muffin with lettuce, onions and French fries. Different soups and luncheon specials are prepared daily.

The Diner features an old-fashioned soda fountain as well as a delicatessen counter offering homemade potato salad, assorted cheeses and cold cuts which may be purchased to take out.

Owners Cassandra Mitchell and Nickie Hamilton have a fresh approach which is symbolized by the well-scrubbed, almost hospital-like decor and white-washed exterior.

———

The Diner, 6476 Washington Street, Yountville 94599 Telephone (707) 944-2626. Hours: Saturday and Sunday, 9 a.m.-3 p.m.; Tuesday-Friday, 6:30 a.m.-3 p.m. Price range: Breakfast, $1.10-$3.00; lunch, $1.35-$3.25. No alcoholic beverages are served. Seating capacity 40.

DOMAINE CHANDON   *Restaurant*

French chef Bernard Lafon manages this intimate fifteen-table restaurant on the grounds of Domaine Chandon Winery. When the weather is fine, visitors may enjoy their meals outdoors on the terraces surrounding the restaurant.

The restaurant features cuisine from the Champagne region and offers an elaborately presented buffet lunchon with terrines, poulet gele, and other dishes complementing sparkling wine.

———

Domaine Chandon, California Drive, Yountville 94599 Telephone (707) 944-8844. Hours: Thursday-Monday, 12 noon-11 p.m. Price: Lunch $5.00; Dinner—$12.00. Corkage $1.50. Reservations suggested. Cards: BA, MC, AE. Seating capacity 60.

JUICED FOR YOU   *Restaurant*

Pam Bright and Mike Pring operate this tiny restaurant in an old railroad car adjacent to Vintage 1870. Their speciality is freshly squeezed juices from fruits and vegetables. The tropical "smoothie" is a delicious meal in itself—a combination of orange, pineapple and tropical juices, yoghurt, honey and ice, whipped to a frothy delight. Sandwiches range from cashew butter and fruit butter to avocado and crab and cen be ordered with a garden mix or tropical fruit salad.

———

Juiced for You, 6503 Washington St., Yountville 94599, Telephone (707) 944-2177. Hours: Tuesday-Sunday, 10 a.m.-5 p.m. Price range: $.95-$2.35. No cards. Seating capacity 16.

GRAPE VINE INN   *Restaurant, Bar*

The Grape Vine Inn has been a Napa Valley institution for forty years. Prominent visibility on Hwy. 29 makes it the busiest restaurant in the area, catering to multitudes of tourists. The large seating capacity makes it possible to absorb swarms of passengers from several Gray Line buses without undue strain. The restaurant specializes in slabs of beefsteak and unusually large salads. The hamburgers on the luncheon menu are enormous half-pound creations on a sesame seed bun served with French fries and antipasto ($2.50) and the lavish salads are recommended to please both the appetite and the purse. The wine list features wines of nine Napa Valley wineries, but the bar is the main attraction.

———

Grape Vine Inn, 7331 St. Helena Hwy., Yountville 94599, Telephone (707) 944-2225. Hours: 11:30 a.m.-10 p.m. daily. Price range: Lunch $1.25-$4.25; Dinner $4.95-$8.95. Corkage fee $1.00. Full bar. Cards: BA, MC, AE. Seating capacity 200.

GROEZINGER WINE COMPANY   *Provisions, Wine*

Behind the brick shopping complex of Vintage 1870 stands the massive Groezinger Winery Stables, out of use since Prohibition. The building has been refurbished and now houses the appropriately named Groezinger Wine Company. Thousands of bottles culled from over one hundred California wineries are attractively displayed on rough-hewn wooden shelves, as well as a representative sampling of one hundred imported wines.

A twenty-foot square topographical map of the Napa Valley hangs on one wall, pinpointing fifty or so local wineries. This thorough approach is typical of proprietor Philip Faight, a young wine enthusiast who is a virtual compendium of enological knowledge.

———

Groezinger Wine Company, Vintage 1870, Yountville 94599, Telephone (707) 944-2331. Hours: Tuesday-Sunday 10 a.m.-5 p.m. Cards: BA, MC.

MAMA NINA'S   *Restaurant*

Although Mama Nina's is a relatively new restaurant, it has already become a favorite of the local populace. Proprietor Lee Kline prepares fresh homemade pasta daily and the Fettuccini all' Alfredo is especially praiseworthy. Other pastas include Tortellini, Tagliarini Pesto, Spaghetti, Gnocchi, and Daglia e' Fieno.

Meals may be ordered a la carte, as a small dinner with soup or salad, or as a full dinner with antipasto tray, soup, salad and dessert, with a glass of sparkling Muscato and coffee. The meals are all served at a liesurely pace.

The soup of the day, usually Lee Kline's variation of minestrone, succeds in being both full-bodied and delicately balanced. The salads of spinach, a combination of mixed greens, and a profusion of walnuts and mushroom slices, are meticulously presented.

Entrees feature a delightful Veal Piccata prepared with lemon and capers; chicken in wine and mushrooms, and Scampi in butter, olive oil, garlic and wine. Also available for the less adventuresome are steak and South Pacific lobster tail.

The wine list has a selection limited to ten Napa Valley wineries but commendably at a $1.50 above shelf price.

Mama Nina's, 6772 Washington St., Yountville 94599, Telephone (707) 944-2112. Hours: Thursday through Monday, 5 p.m.-10 p.m. Price range: $4.95-$10.95. Reservations suggested. Cards: BA, MC, AE. Seating capacity 65.

VINTAGE 1870 *Restaurant, Bar*

The massive complex called Vintage 1870 was once the winemaking domain of Gottlieb Groezinger. Prohibition brought his enterprise to an untimely end, and the structure now houses a myriad of unique shops.

Sally Schmidt operates The Chutney Kitchen where fresh salads and homemade soups are the specialities. Sandwiches include smoked salmon with cream cheese, baked ham, and smoked tongue. For dessert, the cheesecake is excellent. Antiques, bentwood chairs and flowered quilt tablecloths provide a country ambience. Seating is also available on the secluded outside patio.

Sally's daughter, Karen, is the proprietor of the Vintage Cafe, housed in the old railroad station on the property. An outdoor deck facing the entrance of Vintage 1870 provides the perfect location for people-watching while inbibing a cold Heineken beer. The Vintage Cafe specializes in delicious charcoal-broiled hamburgers (considered by many to be the best in the Napa Valley) served on a toasted French roll with a fresh green salad. The espresso machine churns out some enlivening coffee drinks like Mocha cafe. Weekend evenings the restaurant changes into a full bar.

The Chutney Kitchen, Vintage 1870, Yountville 94599, Telephone (707) 944-2788. Hours: Tuesday-Sunday 10 a.m.-5 p.m. Price range: $1.00-$3.50. Cards: BA, MC. Corkage. Seating 75.
The Vintage Cafe, Vintage 1870, Yountville 94599, Telephone (707) 944-2614. Hours: Tuesday-Thursday 10:30 a.m.-5 p.m.; Friday and Saturday, 10:30 a.m.-4p.m., 5 p.m.-midnight. Price: $1.25-$3.00.

VINTAGE 1870 *Provisions*

The Vintage 1870 shopping complex houses two stores which purvey supplies for picnics. The Kitchen Store contains a small delicatessen where several dozen cheeses, cold meats, French bread and bagels are available for sandwich fixings. No alcoholic beverages are available here, but owners Ralph and Joanne Colonna stock numerous organic juices including apple-strawberry and black cherry. Adjacent to the deli is a gourmet section where customers can find imported teas, tins and boxes of crackers, herbs, spices, pickles, jams and other delicacies. The Kitchen Store's own brand of coffee is ground to order.

Tom and Nancy Catterson's shop is facetiously called The Wurst Place in the Napa Valley. They claim to have Northern California's largest assortment of sausages, as well as other quality meats. The Wurst Place stocks everything from pickled pigs' feet to homemade Polish kielbasa, from spicy Mexican chorizo to fresh bratwurst. Local hunters drop by to have their meats custom-smoked or to buy the casings and spices for do-it-yourself sausages.

For the barbeque they offer excellent, aged New York steaks and freshly ground round.

The Kitchen Store, Vintage 1870, Yountville 94599, Telephone (707) 544-8100. Hours: Tuesday-Sunday 10 a.m.-5 p.m. Cards: BA, MC, DC, AE.

The Wurst Place, Vintage 1870, Yountville 94599, Telephone (707) 944-2224. Hours: Tuesday-Sunday, 10 a.m.-5 p.m. No cards.

YOUNTVILLE SALOON   *Restaurant, Bar*

The building which now contains the Yountville Restaurant and Coffee Saloon was constructed at the turn of the century on the site of the town's original livery stable. The decor here is convincingly authentic with rough hewn redwood walls hung with comboy gear and examples of the taxidermist's art. Flamboyant entrepreneur Greg Cochran manages this establishment with the invaluable assistance of Georgia Carmichael. Part of an evening's entertainment is listening to Greg's outrageous tales.

The menu complements the atmosphere by offering entrees such as buffalo stew. Regulars usually order the special of the day. When in season the fresh fish dishes are recommended, particularly salmon or red snapper, served with rice, garden vegetables, French bread and soup or salad. The homemade soup is usually quite good and the pies made by Greg's mom are superb.

Several dozen Napa Valley wines are available here with a few to please even the discriminating palate.

The Yountville Saloon is the only Napa Valley night club that can be recommended. Greg's penchant is for bluegrass and country music and after dinner it is usually crammed to capacity with a footstomping and dancing crowd.

———

Yountville Restaurant and Coffee Saloon, 6480 Washington St., Yountville 94599, Telephone (707) 944-2761. Hours: Dinner, Thursday and Sunday 5:30 p.m.-9:30 p.m.; Friday and Saturday 6:00 p.m.-10:00 p.m. Price range: $2.25-$8.75. No cards. Corkage $2.00. Reservations suggested. Seating 60.

NAPA VALLEY CHEESE CO.   *Restaurant, Provisions*

On the highway just north of Yountville stands a small brick building. Inside a large counter fills one side with an encyclopedic offering of one hundred seventy cheeses from the world over. Types of cheeses and prices appear on a huge chalk board on the wall. Along the window are eight tables cheerfully set with blue tablecloths and flowers. An outdoor area for eating cafe style is under construction, and owners Sandy Morgenstern and Doris Pick are usually on hand slicing cheese or preparing picnic box lunches.

For lunch you can order the cheese board for two ($3.95) served with salami, fresh fruit, French bread and sweet butter. Or perhaps choose a large bowl of homestyle soup served with their unusual tasty provolone and zucchini muffins. The daily cheese-based entree with salad might be roquefort and cream cheese quiche, sauteed chicken breast stuffed with spinach and ricotta cheese, or cheese blintzes topped with fresh strawberries.

The wine list is not large but has been selected with a great deal of care. Wines from over a dozen small Napa Valley vineyards appear here at a cost of a dollar and a half above shelf price.

———

The Napa Valley Cheese Company, 7399 St. Helena Hwy., Oakville, Telephone (707) 944-8333. Lunch: Winter, 11 a.m.-3 p.m.; Summer and weekends, 11:00 a.m.-5:00 p.m. Cheese store hours: 11:00 a.m.-6:00 p.m. Monday-Sunday. Price range: $1.75-$4.50, corkage $1.50. Cards: BA, MC. Seating capacity 32. Reservations accepted.

OAKVILLE GROCERY CO.   *Provisions, Delicatessen*

John Michael's grocery store can be easily identified by the Vintage 1930's Coca Cola billboard on the side of the building. Once inside, a surprise awaits. Lining the shelves are gourmet foods, imported cigarettes, dried fruit and three dozen imported beers. Over two dozen meats and cheeses fill the deli case. This is the place to buy fresh sourdough French bread or have a sandwich made to order. Have a Hagen Dazs ice cream cone while browsing through the wine cellar, which has a small selection of hard-to-get local wines.

———

Oakville Grocery Company, 7856 St. Helena Hwy., Oakville 94562, Telephone (707) 944-2011. Hours: Monday-Sunday, 8 a.m.-6:00 p.m. Open 10 a.m.-5 p.m. on winter weekends. No cards.

POMETTA'S DELICATESSEN   *Restaurant, Provisions*

Mario Pometta uses recipes from his native Italy for his plump ravioli and malfatti, stuffed with a combination of spinach, cheese, garlic, onion, ground beef and spices. The highly recommended pasta is served to your table by Mario or Paula Pometta on tables set up behind the family house. This is a delicatessen serving great sandwiches and barbecued chicken, superb minestrone soup and pasta, as well as salad and pie. No alcohol is served, but guests can bring their own bottles of wine.

———

Pometta's Delicatessen, Hwy. 29 and Oakville Grade, Oakville 94562, Telephone (707) 944-2365. Hours: 7 a.m.-7 p.m. every day. Price range: $.95-$2.25. No cards. Seating capacity: 18 indoors, 3 tables outside.

OAKVILLE PUBLIC HOUSE   *Restaurant, Bar*

Michael Werner's eatery sits at the crossroads of the sleepy whistle-stop of Oakville, population 150.

The relaxed bar is the major attraction and is usually elbow to elbow with locals. Vintage jazz wafts from the jukebox; there is even a small alcove with couches and a coffee table where couples can sip a drink in privacy.

The kitchen here is incredibly tiny and can prepare only a limited number of meals, but plans for expansion are in the works. Friday through Sunday young French chef Jacque Carod creates a number of ever-changing entrees, some of the more memorable of which are Canard a l'Orange, Truite aux Amandes and Langoustines au Cognac. Dinners are served with a warm baguette of French bread, homemade soup (often a delightful cream-based concoction) or a large, crisp salad comprised of a variety of types of lettuce.

Wednesday is "Guest Chef" night. This unusual convention allows armchair gourmets to prepare their specialties for friends and strangers alike in a restaurant setting. Recommended for the daring.

The wine list here, as might be expected in such a small place, conforms to the opinion of the management and may not be to everyone's taste.

———

Oakville Public House, Oakville Crossroad on Hwy. 29, Oakville 94562. Telephone (707) 944-8997. Hours: Dinner, 6 p.m.-10 p.m. Full bar service from 4 p.m. Price range: $5.50-$7.50. No cards. Reservations accepted. Seating capacity 24.

RUTHERFORD SQUARE   *Restaurant, Provisions, Bar*

Rutherford Square consists of The Cottage, a combination ice cream parlor and delicatessen; Rutherford Spirits, a tiny bar, and Mary's Soup Kitchen, a soup and sandwich eatery in the basement of Rutherford Spirits. Uncle Gaylord's Ice Cream Parlor is the outstanding attraction in this complex. Gaylord's purveys old-fashioned ice cream which, as their brochure proclaims, contains no artificial flavors, colors, stabilizers, emulsifiers or chemicals. Flavors available range from molasses walnut to pumpkin raisin The delicatessen in The Cottage offers cheese and cold cuts, sandwiches ($1.65-$2.00), cheese plates, homemade potato salad, some wines and cold imported beer. A few tables allow seating for perhaps twenty people.

A stone's throw away is Rutherford Spirits. This Lilliputian bar holds fifteen people if a few of them stand. Drinks are reasonably priced which probably accounts for the dozens of local farmers who crowd in here daily at 5 p.m. The other attraction is Sandy, the friendly female bartender.

Downstairs among pong and shuffleboard games are six tables and an odd assortment of funky decor. This is Mary's Soup Kitchen where the cuisine is homemade soup, salad and sandwiches ($1.25-$2.75).

———

Rutherford Square, corner of Hwy. 29 and Rutherford Rd., Rutherford, Telephone (707) 963-2317. Hours: The Cottage—Monday-Sunday, 10 a.m.-6 p.m.; Rutherford Spirits — Weeknights, 11 a.m.-7 p.m.; weekends 11 a.m.-10 p.m.; Mary's Soup Kitchen— Monday-Sunday, 11 a.m.- 3 p.m. No cards. Full bar.

THE ABBEY RESTAURANT   *Restaurant*

The Freemark Abbey complex is the busiest tourist stop in Napa Valley and at its center is The Abbey Restaurant.

The really surprising thing about this dinner house is the consistent overall quality of the food, given the enormous volume of meals served. This is largely do to the boundless energy and meticulous attention to detail of proprietor John Pappas.

French sauces are prepared personally every day by Mr. Pappas—and it is the sauces which are responsible for elevating the quality of the food above the level of ordinary.

Luncheon crowds often number two hundred, yet the service is always prompt. The Cannelone Supreme, a spicy chicken, veal and pork-filled crepe, is the most popular entree. The shrimp salad with tomatoes, beets, egg and asparagus is recommended.

Dinners are served in a more relaxed atmosphere and more time is taken in their preparation. The more interesting menu items are Salmon au Champagne, Steak au Poivre Flambe, and Scampi Provencale. For dessert, the most popular choice is homemade baklava.

The wine list, as might be expected, features several wines from Freemark Abbey Winery.

———

The Abbey Restaurant, 3020 St. Helena Hwy., St. Helena 94574, Telephone (707) 963-2706. Hours: Lunch, 12 noon-4 p.m.; Dinner, 5 p.m.-9 p.m. Price range: Lunch, $2.95-$5.25; Dinner, $6.25-$8.75. Corkage $2.00. Reservations suggested. Cards: BA, MC. Seating capacity: 200.

THE BOTTLE SHOP   *Provisions*

Fred Beringer, whose family operated the venerable Beringer Winery for three generations, is the proprietor of the Bottle Shop. Conveniently located on Main Street, the liquor store offers wines from two dozen Napa Valley vintners as well as a selection from neighboring wine-growing regions. This is the best place in St. Helena to stop for chilled wine or imported beer. Huge gold-framed lithographs of famous local wineries are attractively displayed from the walls.

———

The Bottle Shop, 1321 Main St., St. Helena 94574, Telephone (707) 963-3092. Hours: Monday, Wednesday, Thursday: 9 a.m.-9 p.m.; Tuesday, Sunday, 9 a.m.-6 p.m.; Friday, Saturday, 9 a.m.-10 p.m. Cards: BA, MC.

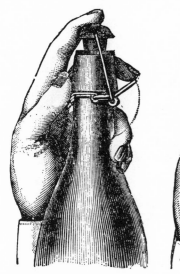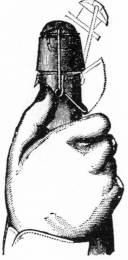

ERNIE'S WINE WAREHOUSE   *Provisions*

Owned by St. Helena resident Ernie Van Asperen of Ernie's liquor store fame, the Wine Warehouse features wines from around the world. On the shelves are several thousand bottles from France's Bordeaux and Burgundy regions. There are wines available from Australia, Italy, Germany, and, of course, California.

Wines from the five dozen California wineries include those sold inexpensively under Ernie's private labels, featuring names like Round Hill, Stone Creek and Rutherford Ranch.

———

Ernie's, 699 St. Helena Hwy., St. Helena 94574. Telephone (707) 963-7888. Hours: 10 a.m.-6 p.m. Monday-Sunday. Cards: BA, MC.

FREEMARK ABBEY GIFT AND GOURMET   *Provisions*

This vendor of victuals is actually located at two separate addresses in the Freemark Abbey complex. The original shop, sandwiched between the Abbey Restaurant and the Hurd Candle Factory, is a general store of gourmet cooking items, including an encyclopedic offering of kitchen utensils from the world over as well as imported delicacies like jams, cookies and teas. Also available is a wide variety of books concerned with wine and food.

At the cellar location across the parking lot, both wine and food are proffered. Counters display four dozen types of cheeses and cold meats which may be purchased by the slice or combined in a standwich with Romain lettuce and Dijon mustard ($1.85).

Salad fixings include shrimp, marinated beans, and asparagus. Fresh quiche is baked daily and sold by the slice ($.95). In addition to French and Armenian bread, crackers, cookies, dried fruit, baklaca and imported foods are included in the culinary selection. Fresh coffee can be ground to order on the premises.

Two dozen Napa Valley wines share the shelves with imported beer, fruit juice and Calistoga water, and a number of them are available chilled, just right for a picnic.

———

Freemark Abbey Gift and Gourmet, 3010 and 3020 St. Helena Hwy., St. Helena 94574. Telephone (707) 963-3833. Hours: Summer: 9:30 a.m.-6 p.m. daily; winter: weekdays, 9:30 a.m.-5 p.m., weekends, 10 a.m.-5 p.m. Cards: BA, MC.

W. F. GIUGNI & SON   *Provisions, Deli*

Third generation owners Bill and Kathy Giugni have retained much of the original atmosphere of this friendly country store. Along with grocery items, Giugni's features homemade chile, minestrone soup, and the house speciality—sandwiches so large they border on the ridiculous ($1.50). In addition, the deli counter displays a variety of goodies including salads, deviled eggs, and carrot cake. Between the infectious humor of the proprietors and the quality of the food, customers usually exit smiling.

W. F. Giugni and Son Grocery Co., 1227 Main St., St. Helena 94574, Telephone (707) 963-3421. Hours: 8 a.m.-6 p.m. daily. No cards.

LORD BRUCE   *Restaurant*

This cheerful bistro has redwood trim, blue-checked tablecloths and Bruegel prints on its whitewashed walls. The luncheon menu offers modest portions of homemade soups, salads and sandwiches. The salad plate is an interesting combination of four salads—marinated bean, tuna, egg and potato—served with French bread ($3.00). Los Hermanos is the house wine and bottles from eight Napa Valley wineries are available in fifths and tenths. As a new feature, Lord Bruce serves dinner Monday through Thursday nights until 8 p.m.

Lord Bruce, 1304 Main St., St. Helena 94574, Telephone (707) 963-3889. Hours: Sunday-Friday, 10 a.m.-6 p.m.; Saturday, 10 a.m.-4 p.m. Price range: $1.25-$3.00. Corkage: $.50-$1.00. No cards.

LA BELLE HELENE   *Restaurant*

La Belle Helene is a tiny provencial French restaurant located in a Nineteenth Century stone edifice on a quiet side street. Snowy-white tablecloths and Oriental rugs and tapestries help create an ambience of informal elegance.

Young owners Gregory Lyons and Gallic charmer Philippe de Tauzia preside over the kitchen and dining room respectively. The ebullient chef takes pride in the fact that everyone in the kitchen is involved with food at a fundamental level of their personality. Their highly individualized approach and an ever-changing menu offer the possibility of supreme success or occasional disappointment.

Menu choices, presented to the table on a chalkboard, might range from veal sauteed with shallots and mushrooms to filet of sole poached in wine with a cream and mushroom sauce. Entrees are served with vegetable garnish and superb cream soup. The entree is followed by a Romaine salad with vinaigrette dressing to cleanse the palate. Special care is taken with the meticulously presented homemade tortes and exotic French pastries.

The thorough wine list offers three dozen carefully selected wines from Napa Valley's finest vineyards.

La Belle Helene, 1345 Railroad Ave., St. Helena 94574 Telephone (707) 963-9984. Hours: Luncheon, 11:30 a.m.-2:30 p.m.; Dinner, 5 p.m.-10 p.m.: Sunday brunch. Price range: Lunch, $2.25-$5.00; Dinner, $8.50-$11.50. Corkage: $3.00. Reservations suggested. No cards. Seating capacity 40.

NAPA VALLEY OLIVE OIL MFG. CO.   *Provisions*

Upon entering the "Olive Oil Factory", owners Osvaldo Particelli and Policarpo Lucchesi are likely to be engaged in lively debate, but unless the visitor speaks Italian, he won't know whether the topic is the price of olives or Roman politics. Olive oil is still produced here as it has been for nearly a century, but the emphasis is on cheese, salami and Italian foods. Two counters are packed with quality cheeses of every size and shape, all at surprisingly low prices.

––––––

Napa Valley Olive Oil Manufacturing Co., 835 McCorkle Ave., St. Helena 94574, Telephone (707) 963-4173. Hours: 8 a.m.-5:45 p.m. daily except holiday. No cards. Seating capacity two picnic tables.

VINTAGE PRODUCE CENTER   *Provisions*

The local produce market is operated by Earl Salingi. Located just off Highway 29, about a mile south of St. Helena, The Vintage Produce Market features everything in fresh fruits and vegetables from avocadoes to zucchini. Cheese, salami, packaged meats and dried fruits line the shelves. A large selection of chilled fruit juices is offered as well as French bread and crackers. Outside, nine picnic tables are available for hungry passersby.

––––––

Vintage Produce Center, 210 Vintage Ave., St. Helena 94574, Telephone (707) 963-9921. Hours: 8 a.m.-6 p.m. daily. Cards: BA. Seating capacity nine picnic tables.

V. SATTUI WINERY   *Provisions*

Daryl and Mirja Sattui are really to be complimented on the tasteful decor and design of their modest new winery on the outskirts of St. Helena. If the Napa Valley had a building code which required new structures to adhere to the area's prevailing 19th Century architectural style (which it regretably does not) the V. Sattui Winery would comply admirably.

Old photographs of Daryl's winemaking grandfather and the equipment used in his trade create an ambience of tradition.

Wines made at this facility are still in the barrels aging; in the meantime, the Sattuis have purchased wines from neighbors. These agreeable wines are available only at the winery at prices which reflect the "lack of middleman" philosophy. Tasting is conducted inside the winery itself, offering the visitor a unique view of a small winery in operation surrounded by crusher, press and various winemaking apparatus.

Provisions offered for sale include ten dozen cheeses, salami, homemade pate, local walnuts, apples, fruit and fresh French bread.

Redwood counters atop old barrels display wine books, crystal glassware, baskets, and gourmet accessories. Patrons are encouraged to picnic among the walnut trees.

––––––

V. Sattui Winery, White Lane, St. Helena 94574, Telephone (707) 963-7774. Hours: 10 a.m.-5:30 p.m., tasting until 4 p.m. only. Cards: BA, MC. Seating capacity 12 picnic tables.

EL FARO   *Restaurant*

There are half a dozen Mexican restaurants in Napa Valley and El Faro is probably the best. This comfortable family cantina is operated by Greg and Carmine Hernandez with ample assistance from daughter Carmine. The recommended Chile Verde is a spicy combination of chunks of beef, green chiles and tomatoes in a rich mole sauce which can be ordered as a full dinner or in a burrito. An order of guacomole or quesadillas make a splendid appetizer.

The Mexican beer selection here is extensive and includes the especially rich Noche Buena.

———

El Faro, 1353 Lincoln St., Calistoga 94515, Telephone (707) 942-4400. Hours: 5 p.m.-9 p.m. Monday-Thursday; 11 a.m.-9 p.m. Friday-Sunday. Price range: $2.10-$4.95. Cards: BA, MC. Seating capacity 50.

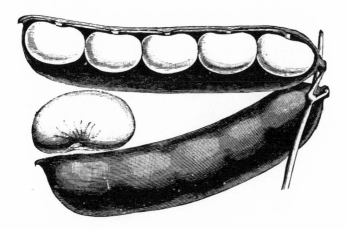

GLEN VISTA   *Restaurant*

Margaret Swegel lives in a cabin about half-way up the arduous Mount St. Helena drive at the two-thousand foot level. Perched atop her house is a small eatery —a roadside oasis. The brief menu is displayed on a plastic Pepsi sign with prices ranging from sixty-five cents to two dollars. This is a one-woman operation with Margaret getting all the credit for the great homemade pies and soups made daily. The breakfast is of the eggs and bacon variety, enhanced by hashbrowns. This is a Margaret's kitchen and she enjoys having people stop by for both food and friendly conservation.

———

Glen Vista, 4421 Lake County Hwy., Calistoga 94515 Telephone (707) 942-4357. Hours: Monday-Friday, 6:30 a.m.-5:30 p.m. Saturday and Sunday, 7:00 a.m.-5:30 p.m. Price range: $.65-$2.00. No alcohol; no credit cards. Seating capacity 20.

PETE'S DELICATESSEN   *Provisions—Delicatessen*

The deli-counter domaine of Pete and Merle Holtzen dispenses some of the most substantial serving portions in the region. The regular sandwich ($1.85) includes lettuce, tomato, onion, and one-quarter pound of meat and/or cheese on your choice of rolls or breads. The smaller student sandwich is a bargain at $.99. For the ravenous, there is the deluxe hot plate ($2.25) consisting of a combination such as Polish sausage, German potato salad, sauerkraut and rye bread. Although Pete's Delicatessen does not feature an extensive choice in wine, the imported beer selection is enormous and may be consumed on the premises.

————

Pete's Delicatessen, 1359 Lincoln Avenue, Calistoga 94515, Telephone (707) 942-6144. Hours: Monday-Saturday, 9:00 a.m.-9:00 p.m.; Sunday, 9:00 a.m.-7:00 p.m. No cards. Seating capacity 60.

TRIPLE "S" RANCH   *Restaurant, Resort*

The century-old Triple "S" Ranch is located high in the Sonoma mountains overlooking a primeval valley. The stately old ranch house is surrounded by a cluster of redwood structures. One of these, the original barn, has been converted into a restaurant where Gladys Hosang cooks her country specialities. Choice beefsteak tops the menu and is generously served with chunky homemade soup, a large iceberg lettuce salad and lots of French bread. The Triple "S" Ranch's special French fried onion rings are said by locals to be the best in the county.

Antique rifles decorate the walls and Country and Western music croons from the jukebox. The Old West is alive and well at Mary Schellenger's Triple "S" Ranch.

The tree-shaded guest cabins look very rustic from the outside, but the interiors are freshly painted and spotlessly clean. The nightly rate of eleven dollars is decidedly a bargain.

The intense summer heat can be dissipated in the cool water of the outdoor pool. Solitude can be enjoyed while hiking on a private mountain trail.

————

Triple "S" Ranch, 4600 Mountain Home Road, Calistoga 94515, Telephone (707) 942-6730. Hours: Open April 1st-December 31st. Monday-Saturday: Dinner, 5 p.m.-10 p.m.; Sunday, p.m.-10 p.m., bar open until 2 a.m. Price range: $4.25-$8.95. Corkage $1.00. Full bar. Cards: BA, MC. Seating capacity 100.

SILVERADO RESTAURANT *Restaurant, Bar*

The effusive country hospitality of the Napa Valley is nowhere more evident than here. Host and sommelier Alex Dierkhising is one of the more knowledgeable wine enthusiasts in the valley and can usually be enticed into a lively enological discussion. The impressive wine list features over one hundred and fifty personally selected bottles all of which are also available for off sale. Wines served with meals are available at a commendable one dollar above retail price. This is a family operation, with brothers Mark and Drake presiding over the kitchen and management respectively.

The bar here is simply the best in the upper valley: a number of interesting wines are always available by the glass or taste. The back bar is a baroque specimen brought around Cape Horn in 1895. Friday and Saturday nights a guitarist or soloist performs.

Wednesday is Zinfandel Beef night. This all-you-can-eat buffet ($4.25) is served steam-table style with fresh vegetables, onion casserole, stewed tomatoes, mashed potatoes, salad and garlic bread. On the regular menu, the Silverado turns out a good steak—Filet Mignon served with maitred' butter. With advance notice, Chef Mark will prepare any specialty.

———

Silverado Restaurant and Tavern, 1374 Lincoln Avenue, Calistoga 94515, Telephone (707) 942-6725. Hours: Monday, 11:00 a.m.-10:00 p.m.; Tuesday-Sunday, 6:00 a.m.-10:00 p.m. Price range: Dinner, $4.25-$8.00; Lunch, $2.00-$4.00; Breakfast, $1.00-$3.00. Corkage fee $1.00. Full bar. Cards: BA, MC. Seating capacity 136. Reservations suggested.

POPE VALLEY PARACHUTE RANCH *Restaurant. Bar*

Isolated Pope Valley lies to the east of St. Helena over Howell Hountain. The entire valley was originally a Mexican land grant given to Julian Pope in 1841. In the center of this sparsely-populated farming community stands Pope Valley Parachute Ranch. All three owners—James Curtis, William Ottley and Edward Matlin—are active practitioners of the ranch's *raison d'etre*: sport parachute jumping. James Curtis is in fact president of the United States Parachutists Association.

Weekends are the ideal time for visitors to vicariously partake in the excitement of parachute jumping. High overhead, airborn jumpers leap from the plane, appearing from the ground as tiny dots until their multicolored parachutes open simultaneously and they slowly sail earthward. (The ranch offers lessons and complete rental services for this aerial art.) Hot-air balloonists also hold gatherings here amid the idyllic pastures and hillsides.

A festive atmosphere usually prevails in the rustic lodge where the restaurant speciality is beefsteaks, which monopolize the dinner menu. For lunch, hamburgers are the appropriate choice.

———

Pope Valley Parachute Ranch, 1996 Pope Valley Road, Pope Valley, Telephone (707) 965-2191. Hours: Thursday—12 noon to 12 midnight; Friday—12 noon to 2 a.m.; Saturday and Sunday—8 a.m. to 2 a.m. Price range: Lunch $1.00-$2.50; dinner $1.95-$7.25. Corkage $1.00. Full bar. Cards: BA, MC. Seating capacity 150.

ISITORS have been travelling Napa's "Wine Road" for over a century enjoying the conviviality and famous hospitality of the region. Robert Louis Stevenson honeymooned here in 1880 and tells the engaging story of his visit in *Silverado Squatters*, penning these inspired words, "The stirring sunlight and the growing vines and the vats and bottles in the cavern made a pleasant music for the mind. Here also the earth's cream was being skimmed and garnered . . . and the wine is bottled poetry."

There is something very special about drinking wine where it is made. After all, wine is a reflection of a mingling of sun, soil, and man. Sipping wine while surrounded by the barrels, crushers and presses, inhaling the winey breath that steals from the walls and ceilings, inextricably binds one to the moment. A visitor may find need of a place to rest, to sort out the tastes and sights he has experienced.

The following information has been provided to aid the overnight guest. The hotels, inns, resorts, spas and campground reviewed offer a variety of lodgings, many amid rural vinyard settings and in keeping with the Napa Valley's time honored tradition of gracious hospitality.

Accommodations in Napa Valley are somewhat limited; therefore, reservations are suggested to insure against disappointment. For visits during the busiest touring months from May to November, reservations thirty to sixty days in advance are advised. For those travelling during winter months, a day's notice should be sufficient.

DOWNTOWN MOTEL   *Motel*

The Downtown Motel is a member of the Western Motel chain and as the name implies is located at the center of Napa's downtown business district about equidistant between the valley's two main arteries, Hwy. 29 and the Silverado Trail. Within easy walking distance of shopping, restaurants, theaters, and post office, the two-story motel complex is immacutely clean and is furnished in motel modern. Extra touches include a heated pool and donuts and coffee at the check-out desk. Harold and Mary Ellingwood manage the facility.

Downtown Motel, 2nd and Coombs Sts., Napa 94558, Telephone (707) 226-1871. Rates: Single $17.00, double $20.00-$22.00. Reservations suggested. Cards: BA, MC. Number of rooms 44.

MOTEL SIX *Motel*

There are over two hundred and forty Motel Six locations throughout the continental United States, each essentially the same as the next. Here in Napa, Motel Six offers fifty-nine spotlessly clean utilitarian rooms with bath, comfortable beds, air conditioning and swimming pool privileges, all at the lowest rates in the area. The popularity of this economical approach necessitates arriving at the motel early or securing reservations in advance. Reservations may either be made in writing or at any Motel Six location.

Motel Six, 3380 Solano Ave., Napa 94558, Telephone (707) 226-1811. Rates: Single $8.95, double $10.95. Television $.50/day. No personal checks or credit cards. Reservations suggested. 59 rooms.

SILVERADO *Resort*

After the Civil War, General John Miller acquired this 1200-acre estate in the eastern foothills of Napa Valley and in 1870 he built a great mansion. As the story goes, he incorporated the original Spanish adobe on the site into the mansion walls. The estate eventually passed from Miller's daughter through two other owners. In 1966, the Hawaii based Amfac Corporation acquired the property and created the pleasure resort of Silverado.

The apartments at Silverado are owned by individuals who allow the management to rent them out when not in use. Each luxurious unit is completely furnished and offers air-conditioning, color television, private bar, fireplace and kitchen. Apartments have either a private patio or a balcony, and are clustered in groups around the five swimming pools.

Silverado also has four attractively appointed conference rooms available to groups of varying size.

Recreational facilities include two challenging 18-hole golf courses and eight tennis courts (each with permanent viewing stands).

For convenience, guests may luncheon in the Mixed Grill where the salad bar is a popular attraction, or dine in the main lodge overlooking a panorama of trees and mountains.

Silverado, 1600 Atlas Peak Road, Napa 94558, Telephone (707) 255-2970. Room rates: $35.00-$92.00, single or double. Full bar service. Reservations suggested. Cards: BA, MC, AE, DC. Number of rooms 190.

BURGUNDY HOUSE   *Inn*

The Burgundy House was constructed of twenty-two-inch-thick fieldstone walls and massive handhewn posts and timbers by Charles Rouvegneau over a century ago. Present owners Bob and Mary Keenan bought the building in 1974 to use as an antique shop with display rooms upstairs. One by one, the rooms were converted to accommodate overnight guests and the inn became a reality.

The six bedrooms and three bathrooms are colorfully furnished with an eclectic grouping of antiques from various periods. Each silk-sheeted antique bed is covered with a cozy-looking quilt. On a nearby nightstand rests a carafe of wine encircled by wine glasses. The view from bedroom windows is of vineyards stretching to the nearby hills.

Downstairs guests may play billiards on an antique pool table or relax by the fire and chat with loquacious host Mary Keenan. Continental breakfasts included in the room rate are served around the big pine table in the hearthroom.

Several blocks away, the Keenans also rent two rooms in a homespun cottage. A luxurious six-room inn is being constructed on this site and will feature sunken Roman baths, fireplaces and queen size beds.

———

Burgundy House, 6711 Washington St., Yountville 94599, Telephone (707) 944-2711 Rates: $35.00-$40.00 single; $38.00-$45.00 double. Rates include wine and breakfast. Reservations recommended. Cards: BA, MC, AE. Number of rooms 14.

MAGNOLIA HOTEL   *Inn, Restaurant*

The Magnolia Hotel traces its origins as an inn to the year 1873. After years of disuse, the brick and stone hostelry was rejuvenated by Ray and Nancy Monte and their children in 1966. The entire structure was extensively renovated in keeping with the original century old architecture.

All six cozy guest rooms are furnished differently with antique decor, using brass beds, marble-topped washstands and dressing tables. Victorian floral-print carpet runs throughout all three floors of the venerable establishment. In addition, each room has such modern conveniences as air-conditioning and a private bath with shower and tub.

There is even a sunken jacuzzi bath in the enclosed redwood patio.

Breakfasts are served in the dining room around a large oak table and might consist of orange juice, rounds of French toast topped with Malvasia wine syrup, bacon and steaming hot coffee, served by ever-gracious host Ray Monte.

Dinners are offered at the hotel Thursdays through Saturday on two levels: upstairs in a cheerful room with French windows and stone fireplace, and downstairs in a candlelit wine cellar.

———

Magnolia Hotel, 6529 Yount St., Yountville 94599, Telephone (707) 944-2056. Room rates: $40.00 double, includes breakfast for two. Restaurant hours: Thursday-Sunday, 7 p.m.-9 p.m. Price $15.00. Corkage $2.00. Cards: BA, MC, AE. Reservations suggested.

CHALET BERNENSIS   *Inn*

A native of Bern, Switzerland, pioneer John Thomann carved the name Chalet Bernensis into his stone entry gate, a name which simply means "from Bern". The striking gingerbread structure was originally part of the Sutter Home Winery property next door. This Napa Valley landmark, now owned by Jack and Essie Doty, houses an antique shop and gallery on the main floor and a European-style boarding house upstairs.

There are only five guest rooms, each furnished with Victorian period antiques reminiscent of an age generations removed from our own. The intimate rooms contain elements of the original decor and one definitely gets the impression of staying as overnight guests in a private home. This feeling is accentuated by the fact that there are only two bathrooms which are shared by the guests.

The inn is conveniently located on St. Helena Hwy. one mile south of the St. Helena town limits and within walking distance of four winery tasting rooms. The rates are the least expensive inn-style accommodations in the valley and they include a hearty continental breakfast served in the dining room until 10 a.m.

A small garden in back of the chalet provides a picnic area for guests of the Doty family.

———

Chalet Bernensis, 225 St. Helena Hwy., St. Helena 94574, Telephone (707) 963-4423. Rates: $30.00, includes continental breakfast. Open daily. Number of rooms 5. Cards: BA, MC, AE. Reservations suggested.

EL BONITA   *Motel*

New owners Jim and Rita Ryan have been busily painting and remodelling since they purchased the El Bonita Motel, located on Hwy. 29 just south of St. Helena. In the courtyard surrounding the pool are sixteen modest but hospital rooms, each with shower, air conditioning and television. Six more luxurious garden rooms are located in a wooded area at the rear of the property. These secluded units, each tastefully decorated in a different colonial style, have sliding glass doors that open onto a picnic-tabled lawn, as well as an optional kitchenette which may be rented for an additional charge of $3.00 per day.

———

El Bonita Motel, 195 Main St., St. Helena 94574, Telephone (707) 963-3216. Rates: Single occupancy, $15.00-$22.00; double, $17.00-$26.00. Number of rooms 22. Reservations suggested. Cards: BA, MC.

MEADOWOOD SUBURBAN CLUB   *Resort*

This semi-private club is nestled in a secluded canyon outside of St. Helena. The road winds along a shady creekbed, strewn with moss-covered boulders and ferns. Stands of oak, madrone and fir diffuse the sunlight, creating patterns on the lichen-covered rock walls of this old estate.

On a grassy knoll at a wide place in the canyon are three tennis courts and swimming pool, complete with bath house, refreshment stand and umbrella covered tables.

On the hillside above is a cluster of seven treetop chalets offering the privacy of a mountain retreat. Each of the roomy redwood chalets has a kitchenette and sunny outside deck. The units are available on a daily or weekly rental basis at rates which include the morning San Francisco newspaper and a continental breakfast.

The road ends at the clubhouse where guests can luncheon overlooking the nine-hole golf course and sip wines produced by member vintners. Reservations for non-member guests are required.

————

Meadowood Suburban Club, 900 Meadowood Lane, St. Helena 94594, Telephone (707) 963-3646. Hours: Lunch, Tuesday-Sunday, 11 a.m.-2:30 p.m.; Dinner, Friday and Saturday, 7 p.m.-9 p.m. Price range: Lunch $2.25-$3.25; Dinner $6.75-$10.25. Corkage $1.50. Full bar service. Room rates: $21.00-$57.00 (rates vary according to the season and the day of week). No cards. Reservations suggested.

WINE COUNTRY INN   *Inn*

Before building their country inn, Ned and Marge Smith spent a great deal of time and effort researching the traditional inns of New England. A hillside building site near Freemark Abbey was selected, not only for its exceptional view, but also its proximity to food and other provisions. Construction was totally a family effort—even Marge's octogenarian mother contributed crewel work and stitchery. Craftsmen sons Jim and Doug were responsible for the stonemasonry and woodworking. The aesthetically pleasing result is a credit to the Smith family and a tribute to the 19th Century architecture of the Napa Valley.

Each of the fifteen rooms at the inn has a fireplace and wall-to-wall carpeting, and is individually decorated with antique furnishings, refurbished by members of the family. Antique beds, some crowned with canopies, have been skillfully adapted to accommodate queen-size mattresses. Handmade quilts are the perfect final touch to these unique rooms. Every room has a view; some have private balconies, and others, patios leading to the lawn where guests may picnic among wildflowers. In addition, a generous continental breakfast is served in the Early American common room.

The Smiths extend a warm welcome to wine lovers, and to weary travelers.

————

Wine Country Inn, 1152 Lodi Lane, St. Helena 94574 Telephone (707) 963-7077. Rates: $35.00-$38.00 includes continental breakfast for two. No children, no pets. Open daily except December 22-27. Reservations suggested. Number of rooms 15.

BOTHE-NAPA VALLEY STATE PARK   *Campground*

In 1872, Dr. Charles Hitchcock bought a thousand acres and built a home "Lonely" beside Ritchie Creek which tumbles from the slopes of nearby Diamond Mountain. His unconventional daughter Lillie Coit and her many friends from San Francisco's elite enjoyed lively social gatherings here contributing to its later popularity as a vacation spot. Reinhold Bothe acquired the property in 1929 for a community campground. It became a state park in 1960.

The park offers camping, picnicking, and swimming (lifeguard on duty throughout the summer season). A number of hiking trails in the 1242-acre park wind off into the surrounding hills whose elevations reach 2000 feet. A variety of native fauna can be observed by the watchful hiker among the stands of coastal redwood and forests of Douglas fir, oak, madrone and other native trees.

There are thirty-five developed campsites on the grounds, each with table and barbecue. Restrooms with hot-water showers and laundry tubs are nearby. Summer campfire programs discussing the plants, wildlife and history of Napa Valley are a regular well attended feature.

Campsites can be reserved during the busiest season between May and September at any Ticketron outlet in California.

———

Bothe-Napa Valley State Park, 3601 St. Helena Hwy. Calistoga 94515, Telephone (707) 942-4575. Price: $4.00/night. Reservations recommended. No. of campsites 35.

CALISTOGA SPA   *Spa, Motel*

Two outdoor mineral pools at the Calistoga Spa are open to the public from 8 a.m. to 9 p.m. every day of the year. The open air pool is 100°F; the other is a 105°F covered octagonal pool with benches, whirlpool jets and a cool water fountain. The pools are surrounded by garden greenery and lounge chairs perfect for relaxing on starlit summer evenings. Somehow, the night-time ambience created here is almost tropical in nature.

The indoor bath facilities are similar to those found in other Calistoga spas. Available are mud bath, whirlpool, steam, blanket sweat and massage. In addition an outdoor Olympic-size pool (88°) is open to the public during the summer from 10 a.m. to 6 p.m.

Most of the thirty-five rooms at the spa are of very recent construction with spacious wood-panelled interiors and open beam ceilings. The seven older units make a reasonable economy accommodation at $16.50 per night, lacking only shower facilities. All rooms, regardless of age, are equipped for light housekeeping with kitchenettes. All guests have free use of both the indoor and outdoor hot pools.

———

Calistoga Spa, 1006 Washington Street, Calistoga 94515, Telephone (707) 942-6269. Rates: Single $19.00, double $21.00. Treatments available: mud bath with mineral tub, whirlpool, steam and blanket wrap, $8.00; mineral bath with whirlpool, steam and blanket wrap, $5.50; massage with steam, $9.00. Reservations suggested. Cards: BA, MC. Number of rooms 35.

DR. WILKENSON'S   *Spa, Motel*

"The Napa Valley with its wine grapes and health spas is a very European slice of life," exclaims Dr. Wilkenson, who established this hot springs here twenty-five years ago.

Once in the lobby of Dr. Wilkenson's spa, one gets the distinct impression of being in a private European medical clinic. Attendants are on hand to offer assistance with the available treatments: mineral tub, hot mud bath, whirlpool, massage, chiropractic adjustment or colonic irrigation. Physical therapy is by a registered therapist. Near the bath house is an indoor, hot mineral pool, equipped with hydrojets. Sliding glass doors open onto an enclosed sunny patio.

Rooms are available for daily or weekly stays in units that fulfill all the requirements for quality modern motel accommodations, including color television and air conditioning. Rooms with kitchens are also available for an additional nightly charge of $3.50. Guests have use of the indoor jacuzzi mineral bath for $1.00 daily charge.

Dr. Wilkenson's Hotel Springs, 1507 Lincoln Ave., Calistoga 94515, Telephone (707) 942-4102. Rates: Single $20.00-$21.00, double $22.00-$25.00. Treatments available: mudbath with steam and blanket wrap, $8.00; mineral bath with steam and blanket wrap, $6.00; massage with mineral bath, $14.00; massage only, $9.00; chiropractic adjustment, $10.00; colonic, $14.00. Cards: BA, MC. Reservations suggested. Number of rooms 33.

GOLDEN HAVEN   *Motel, Spa*

The Golden Haven is located in a quiet residential section, three blocks from Calistoga's main street, and a few minutes' walk from the city's tennis courts. The twenty-eight room complex has a very modern appearance and is kept in excellent repair by Amelia and Matthew Guisto. The newest units feature queen-size beds, skylights, color television and refrigerators. The housekeeping units come complete with a full kitchen. Couches in the living room area convert into single beds. All the rooms are air conditioned and radiant heat is supplied by the constantly circulating hot water. Mineral water is available on tap in the bathrooms.

All guests have use of the naturally heated indoor mineral pool (80°) and sunken bubble pool (90°). It is a short stroll to a separate building at the end of the drive where couples may enjoy the only private jacuzzi whirlpool bath in Calistoga.

During your stay, be sure to make an appointment with masseuse Kathryn Quinn. Kathryn is a specialist in reflexology, a zone therapy in which the underlying principle is that nerve endings in the feet correspond to different organs and muscles in the body. One-half hour of foot massage is guaranteed to reduce tension.

———

Golden Haven, 1713 Lake Street, Calistoga 94515, Telephone (707) 942-6793. Room rates: $17.00-$22.00 single; $26.00-$30.00 double. Open daily. Treatments: intensive massage, ½ hour-1¼ hours, $10.00-$20.00; foot reflexology, $8.00; private jacuzzi bath, $3.00/¼ hour. Cards: BA, MC, AE. 28 rooms. Reservations recommended.

MOUNTAIN HOME RANCH   *Resort, Restaurant, Bar*

Ludwig and Emma Orth homesteaded this isolated mountain resort in 1913. The first guests slept in candlelit tents and ate on the back porch of the proprietors' home. Today, the Orth family still owns the ranch; guests can choose their accommodations from very rustic summer cabins to modern cottages.

Mountain Home Ranch offers a leisurely vacation setting amid 350 forested acres. Trails meander along the foothills where guests will find a redwood-shaded creek and a lake for fishing. Recreational facilities include swimming pools and a tennis court.

The main lodge houses a relaxed bar and two dining rooms. Meals for guests staying here on the American plan are included in the rates, but on weekends non-residents can partake of the excellent cuisine such as fried chicken prepared from Grandpa Orth's original recipe, served with relish plate, homemade soup, a large and imaginatively prepared salad, fresh vegetables and dessert ($5.50). Also available on the dinner menu are beef rouladen and the popular prime rib.

———

Mountain Home Ranch, Mountain Home Ranch Road, Calistoga 94515, Telephone (707) 942-6616. Hours: Friday-Saturday, 6 p.m.-10 p.m.; Sunday, 2 p.m.-8 p.m. Price range: $4.95-$8.50. Corkage $1.00. Room rates: American plan: $16.50-$24.50 single; $27.00-$38.00 double; European plan: $16.00-$18.00, single; $18.00-$20.00, double. Reservations suggested. Full bar. Cards: BA, MC. Number of rooms 21.

NANCE'S HOT SPRINGS   *Spa, Motel*

Charles Nance worked at the Pacheteau Hot Springs until 1917, then built his own spa on an adjoining piece of property, with the help of partner Frank Hughes. Today, Hughes' son, Frank, Jr., and wife, Cathy, run the family business with the help of their children. Familiar faces return year after year to enjoy the healthful waters.

The spa facilities at Nance's date back sixty years and offer the traditional mud bath, mineral tub, sulphur steam cabinet, massage and blanket sweat. The large indoor jacuzzi pool is open from 8 a.m. to 10 p.m. The bath house is open to the public every day of the year.

Nance's Hot Springs is located in downtown Calistoga adjacent to the glider port where pilots and tourists alike soar heavenword in engineless planes on the updrafts created by the surrounding mountains.

Nance's is also much more home-spun in its appearance, avoiding the hospital-like features of some of its neighbors. The vintage motel facilities are clean and in good repair. The kitchenette in each room is a one-piece unit combining stove, oven and refrigerator.

———

Nance's Hot Springs, 1614 Lincoln Avenue, Calistoga 94515, Telephone (707) 942-6211. Hours: 8 a.m.-4 p.m. daily. Treatments: mud, mineral bath, steam and blanket sweat, $8.00; with massage, $14.00. Mineral bath, steam and blanket sweat, $6.00; with massage, $12.00 Massage, $10.00. Room rates: $17.00, single; $19.00, double. Cards: BA, MC. Reservations recommended. 24 units.

PACHETEAU'S CALISTOGA HOT SPRING *Spa, Lodging*

This venerable establishment rests on the site of Sam Brannan's original bath houses. Century-old palms line the circular drive through the grounds. The Pacheteau family acquired this property from Senator Leland Stanford sixty years ago, and the present bath facilities date back to that period. In the central lobby, guests are segregated—men to the left, women to the right—and led to the bath quarters from which wafts the distinct sulphur smell of the vaporous waters. Available are sulphur steam cabinet, hot mineral tub, mud bath (prepared from the black volcanic ash on the grounds) and massage, as well as a 90° mineral-water, outdoor Olympic-sized pool (April-October).

There are fourteen housekeeping cottages on the grounds. Each unit has three very clean rooms including a bedroom with twin beds, a full kitchen and a bathroom with shower. The only thing that gives away the age of the units is the slightly antiquated kitchen appliances. The cottages are quite far apart and a good distance from the road, giving a feeling of seclusion and privacy. Overnight guests have free use of the pool.

———

Pacheteau's Calistoga Hot Springs, 1712 Lincoln Avenue, Calistoga 94515, Telephone (707) 942-5589. Bath hours: 8 a.m.-3 p.m. daily. Treatments: mud bath with mineral tub, sulphur steam, blanket wrap, $7.50; with massage, $15.00. Steam bath with mineral tub, blanket wrap, $7.50, with massage, $13.50. Massage and shower, $10.00. Outdoor pool, $2.50/day. Room rates: $20.00 single or double. Cards: BA, MC. Reservations recommended. 14 rooms.

WARDWAY MOTEL *Motel*

Friendly hosts Ben and Irene Day offer old-fashioned hospitality in a quiet location two blocks from Calistoga's main street, within walking distance of the entire town including stores and spas. There are sixteen freshly painted and carpeted units with kitchenettes. The accommodations are as clean and modern as any in Calistoga, lacking only the "extras" such as mineral pools and color television offered by the neighboring spas.

———

Wardway Motel, 1202 Pine St., Calistoga 94515, Telephone (707) 942-6829. Rates: Single $14.00, double $16.00. Open daily. Reservations suggested. Cards: BA, MC. Number of rooms 16.

ROMAN SPA *Spa, Lodging*

The Roman Spa, formerly Piner's Hot Springs, is undergoing a facelift at the hands of new owners Max and Gena Quast. The old and the new facilities co-exist here in democratic fashion with the rates based on the age of the accommodations. The lowest cost for two people is $16.00; the highest, $24.00.

———

Roman Spa, 1300 Washington Street, Calistoga 94515, Telephone (707) 942-4441. Treatments: Jacuzzi and massage, $14.00; one hour massage, $12.00; thirty minute massage, $7.00; colonics, $16.00; jet bath, massage and therapy, $14.00; jacuzzi, $6.50. Room rates: New units $24.00 double; Original units, $16.00 single, $18.00 double. Cards: BA, MC. Reservations recommended. 19 rooms.

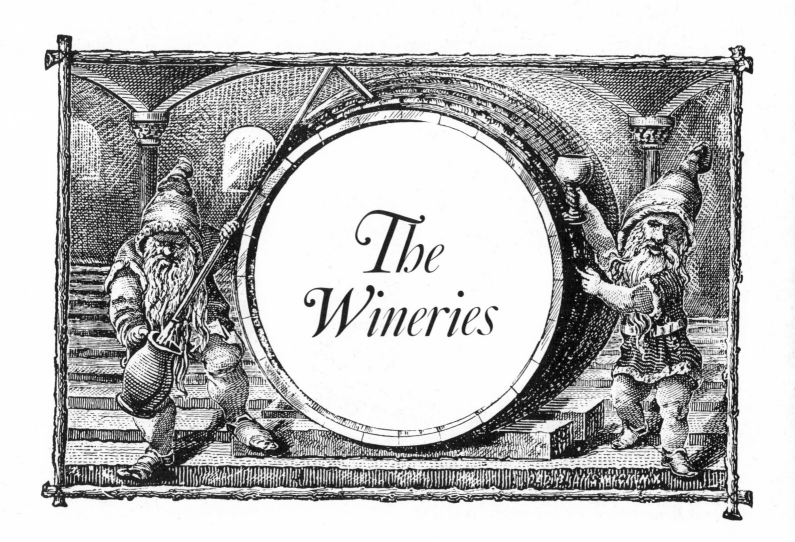

The Wineries

Carneros Creek Winery

Carneros Creek Winery is situated beneath the slopes of Miliken Peak, and is the southernmost winery in the valley. The owners, Balfour and Anita Gibson, founded the winery in 1971.

Los Carneros (the sheep) is the famous cool winegrowing area close to San Pablo Bay, where the early ripening varieties of grapes are particularly at home. The marine intrusion and fog factor play a vital role in the development of high quality varietal fruit. With cooler summers away from valley heat, Pinot Noir, Chardonnay and White Riesling grapes are able to stay on the vine in this area longer, retaining their balance of sugar and acid, and thus developing more character.

The basic premise of this winery is to help establish vineyards and plant the right varieties at the right places to achieve maximum results in the wine. This will require the diligence of Francis Mahoney, the winemaker, in overseeing the vineyard operations during all phases of pruning, cultivation and picking in this low Region I area.

Mahoney was an employee of the Gibsons in their importing business, and the three decided to establish a vineyard and begin making wine. He was already a home winemaker, with experience from working at Mayacamas, and he attacked the project with enthusiasm. "To put in ten acres of vineyard with your own hands helps to destroy the romantic view," he comments, "and if that doesn't do it, then there is the hard, tiring work and long hours at winery chores that go on seven days a week."

This grand experiment will be a five year program, carefully planned, with results yet to be seen. The 1974 crush includes Cabernet Sauvignon grapes from five different locations, and as Mahoney says, "only the years can determine the future of these wines." It is sure to be an interesting experiment, worthy of his best efforts to seek the finest wine obtainable. Mahoney is determined to try for better and better wines each year, as his expertise and experience increase, and the reputation of Carneros Creek Vineyards is expected to increase accordingly.

The winery building, completed in 1973, is constructed of Sonoma block and poured solid. The dimensions are 40 by 80 feet, and the roof is topped with six inches of styrofoam, which supplies efficient insulation. All of the fermenting is done outside in stainless steel refrigerated fermenters, designed at a pitch of three inches to the foot to allow for ease of movemnt of the pomace.

The ultimate goal of the winery is to achieve a volume of 7500 cases a year. There are less than ten acres at the winery site, recently budded to Pinot Noir, which will augment the other grapes that will be purchased. Cabernet Sauvignon, Pinot Chardonnay, Zinfandel and Pinot Noir will be made and sold by the winery in the near future, with emphasis on the Appelation and district recognition of individual vineyards.

There is no tasting or sales at the winery, but an advance appointment will secure the interested visitor a delightful tour, and some good "wine talk".

Mount Veeder Winery

This small, pleasantly situated winery is located on the slopes of Mt. Veeder at a level of from about 1000 to 1400 feet. It is the old Moyer place, purchased in 1963 by Attorney Michael Bernstein and his wife Arlene as a summer home.

In the beginning, the Bernsteins bought the ranch as a place to get away from the bustle of city life. As time went on, the area became more and more attractive to them, and they wanted to spend more of their time there.

Original planting was a prune orchard. For several years they refreshed from the hectic pace by training, spraying and pruning trees, picking and marketing the crop. A log cabin on the property, built by the former owner from material on the land—rocks and trees—has proved to be a comfortable home for Mike and Arlene, and has undergone only minor changes and renovations in their years of residence.

In 1965 they planted a few grapevines in areas not taken up by prune trees. This continued through the next few years, and by 1968 they began taking out prunes and planting grapes. The planting is now complete and bearing—13 acres of Cabernet Sauvignon, the remaining 7 acres of Zinfandel and Chenin Blanc.

During these busy years of planting vineyard, Mike and Arlene Bernstein worked side by side, with their own hands preparing the land, planting and cultivating the vines, watering them during long hot summers until they were well on their way to fruitful maturity. There was a light crop in 1971—and after that, as Mike remarks, "the thing just evolved naturally. We saw that this was what we had been looking for—a quality of life that we had not known before." The first wines were made in the Bernstein home, a 1970 Cabernet Sauvignon. The results encouraged them to think of building the winery, which was begun in 1972.

During these first years, Kimball Giles, North Coast winemaker, worked with the Bernsteins on designing the winery and making the first wines. Mike himself has now given up his law practice and assumed fulltime winemaking duties, along with winegrowing and winery management.

Arlene, from the first, has worn many hats, filling in where she was needed during the busy, happy years of launching the enterprise and getting it established among the fine small wineries of Napa Valley.

There are several innovative practices in use at Mt. Veeder Winery, among them the efficient use of gravity for moving wines from fermenter to press. Although the building is about the size of a one-bedroom home, with maximum capacity of 2000 cases, the Bernsteins have taken pride in giving it the best equipment available, including a small but complete lab.

Ownership is a limited partnership, with the Bernsteins as general partners and other investors involved in a limited capacity.

Interested persons are asked to write or phone ahead before coming to the winery, for all visiting is by appoinment only. As Arlene explains, the owners are also the work force.

Mayacamas Vineyards

MAYACAMAS

Vintage 1968

Late Harvest
ZINFANDEL

ALCOHOL 17% BY VOLUME
PRODUCED AND BOTTLED BY
Mayacamas Vineyards
NAPA, CALIFORNIA

The Mayacamas Winery is reached· by a road winding through the wooded mountain country separating Napa and Sonoma Valleys. High on the slopes of Mt. Veeder, an extinct volcano, the winery setting is magnificent, and the view of valley and hills has an untamed grandeur that is unforgettable. Deer, cougar and bobcats are resident in the area; Mayacamas was the name a valley Indian tribe gave to the mountain range and is said to mean "howl of the mountain lion."

The winery is ten miles northwest of Napa, at 1900 feet elevation. John Henry Fisher, a San Francisco pickle merchant, from Stuttgart, built the native stone winery in 1889, and planted the hillside vineyards. His attempt at growing grape varieties such as Zinfandel and "Sweetwater" is captured in "The Vineyard," written by that master wine country writer, Idwal Jones. The story depicts the mountain vine growers of the time with warmth and honesty. They were a breed apart, a hardier lot than those who grew vines on the valley floor. The statement "He who plants a vine becomes entangled in its branches," is never more appropriate than when applied to the old-time mountain vineyardists.

Fisher sold the property at the turn of the century. It was allowed to run down during Prohibition, and was not reclaimed until Jack and Mary Taylor purchased it in 1941. The distillery building became a comfortable home, and the winery, formerly called "Mt. Veeder Vineyards," was renamed Mayacamas.

During the next 20 years, the Taylors replanted the vineyards to Chardonnay and Cabernet Sauvignon at great expense and endless toil. This couple gave the area a legacy of fine wines through their extraordinary foresight and dedication to the vine. They left a mark on the land and on many palates, for their wine had the strength and vigor of mountain grown vines.

By 1961 the management of Mayacamas was left in younger hands. The Taylors, commuting between Napa and New York, began offering stock to their customers at $10 a share. This enabled Mayacamas to double its small capacity, and the Taylors made it available in exclusive restaurants and wine shops, where it won recognition for excellence.

Bob Travers, a Stanford graduate, and six limited partners took control of Mayacamas in 1968. He did not come to the winery as a neophite, as many did in that era. His research over the years included trips to Europe and enology courses at UC Davis. An apprenticeship at Heitz Cellars gave him valuable experience. Now he makes his home in the converted distillery, with his wife and children. In the interest of pursuing excellence he has limited offerings to three wines, hoping, by doing so, to improve the already fine wines traditionally made at Mayacamas. His Late Harvest Zinfandel has been widely acclaimed.

He continues to plant, wrestle with rocky hillside soil, losing one grape stake in three to its resistance. Upholding the precedent of making great wine that began in 1889 is of utmost importance to this dedicated winemaker.

Trefethen Vineyards

The handsome, pumpkin-colored old building glimpsed through trees above Napa at Oak Knoll Ave. has intrigued the imagination of many valley visitors. None found it more interesting than Gene Trefethen, who bought the property and the surrounding vineyards in 1968. The winery stands on the site of the Oak Knoll Vineyards which were originally planted by Napa pioneer Joseph Osborn in the 1850's.

The winery building is three stories high, built in 1886 for the then handsome sum of $1500, exclusive of materials. Architect Hamden McIntyre, already building a reputation for winery design, created the plans for owners James and George Goodman. It is an imposing structure, with huge timbered walls, built to last of 3 x 12's, 2 x 14's, and 12 x 14's, walls and ceilings lined with tongue-and-grooved redwood. The winery was operated during the 1880's as Eschol Vineyards. It is one of the few wooden wineries built before the turn of the century which has not been a victim of fire.

The Trefethen family considers it a first priority to retain the character of the old building, while giving it the most modern winemaking and aging equipment. Trefethen winery was launched by Gene, his son John, and Tony Baldini. John manages the winery, planned and supervised its refurbishing and equipping, and also makes the wine. Tony has a natural affinity for the soil, a dedication to caring for it, enhancing it, seeing it yield its fruits. He is responsible for the grapes on which the Trefethen reputation is being founded. His skill and care are apparent in the acres of well-kept vineyard on the estate.

In 1973, a fortunate meeting between Trefethen and the French firm Moet-Hennessey resulted in agreement to share the Trefethen winery with Moet while the latter designed and built its permanent facility. The arrangement has worked well; Moet finishes crushing its low-sugar grapes for sparkling wine just as Trefethen readies for its own crush.

All Trefethen wines are estate bottled. The grapes make the wine, Trefethen believes; using superior grapes is the only route to superior wine. They look to Baldini to produce these.

After careful study and research, and the making of experimental lots of wine, Trefethen decided on the varieties of wine the vineyards can best produce. These include Chardonnay, White Riesling and Cabernet Sauvignon. Winemaker John Trefethen learns as he goes, adapting varieties to the different micro-climates on the 600-acre vineyard. After more work, more experimental wines made, aged and studied, a fourth variety will be added.

Recently added to the staff is enologist David Whitehouse, a UC Davis graduate with some years' experience in another prestigious winery with aims and purposes similar to those at Trefethen. He looks to Whitehouse to help keep them abreast of new winemaking techniques and methods, and to assist in general winery work.

Clos du Val Vineyards

This new winery, off Silverado Trail near Chimney Rock Golf Course, at Yountville, is constructed of aggregate and timber, with arched stained glass windows. There is a red concrete tile roof, and the architecture by Keith & Associates of Santa Rosa is reminiscent of old California in the days of George Yount.

The setting is at the southeastern end of Napa Valley. The site is rural and scenic, with a backdrop of low foothills covered with spreading oaks, behind these the jagged outcroppings of Stag's Leap. The valley narrows here, bringing the western hills into a feeling of intimacy with the site, and at the rear and sides are the greens of the golf course. Around the winery are the vineyards of Cabernet Sauvignon and Zinfandel grapes, the only two varieties from which the wines will be made.

A young Frenchman, Bernard Portet, is winemaker and manager, and one of the limited partners owning the winery. He came to this country in early 1972, and crushed the first of the winery's Cabernet and Zinfandel that fall. During the first years of its existence, the winery used as its base of operations the old Occidental Winery in a nearby location. This is an interesting structure, built by T. L. Grigsby in 1878, on land that was part of the Yount grant from Mexico. It will continue to be used as a storage facility.

Young Portet, a member of a French winemaking family, is a graduate of Montpelier University with a degree in viticulture, enology and agronomy. He comments that Napa Valley was chosen for the winery "because it has great potential." Of all the wine growing regions of the world he has seen, this seemed the most favorable spot to launch the winery enterprise. "There are very good wines made here, with lots of finesse and character. Besides that, the valley is a good place to live and work—there is a certain ambience here." He speaks English perfectly, with little accent.

The winery building is 150 feet by 90 feet; it is planned that it will be a small winery, with no more than 14,000 or 15,000 cases—30,000 to 40,000 gallons, made each year.

As with several of the other new valley wineries, no visitor facilities are at Clos du Val, and none are planned for the future. "This is a working winery," says Portet. There is not a retail room at the winery, at present, but one is planned. Wines will be marketed through retail stores.

The 1972 Zinfandel and Cabernet Sauvignon were released in the fall of 1974, only two years old, and capable of further development through judicious cellaring. The wines are drinkable, says the winemaker, but can be improved by further aging. It depends on personal preference, he remarks, how much more age is desirable.

Speaking of the future, Portet looks forward to a long life of living and making good wine in Napa Valley, but he remains a true Frenchman—"When I retire, I will probably want to go back to live in France," he says.

Stag's Leap Wine Cellars

1973
Johannisberg Riesling
Napa Valley
Birkmyer Vineyards

STAG'S LEAP WINE CELLARS

Produced & bottled by Stag's Leap Wine Cellars, Napa, Calif. • Alcohol 12% by volume

Stag's Leap Wine Cellars nestles at the foot of a wooded knoll about a mile north of Chimney Rock Golf Course on Silverado Trail. The winery building is simply designed in traditional California style, and stands in a grove of spreading oaks. It is equipped with stainless steel fermenters and French and Jugoslavian oak cooperage, and is known among winemakers as a model of efficient design.

The 44-acre vineyard and the 70-year-old residence, now the home of the Warren Winiarski family, overlook the historic Stag's Leap Ridge, a series of rocky crags that has become a valley landmark. There is even a legendary stag associated with the area.

Warren Winiarski is general partner and winemaker at Stag's Leap Wine Cellars. He came to California in 1964 to perfect his education in the art and disciplines of winemaker, first with Lee Stewart at the original Souverain Cellars, later with the Robert Mondavi Winery. During these and subsequent years, he found and purchased the site for the winery's home Cabernet and Merlot vineyards.

The entire Winiarski family has been involved in the vineyard and winery operations from the beginning. The three children have always had chores suited to their abilities, and are learning about winemaking from the vineyard up. Barbara Winiarski supervises winery publicity, hospitality, and acts as expert taster of the wines during their journey through the stages of their development from fermenter to bottle.

The first Cabernet from the home vineyard was crushed in 1972, and the winery was completed the following year. It is designed for a yearly production of approximately 15,000 cases—the most Warren feels he can handle and carefully supervise all phases of production.

The winery also produces Johannisberg Riesling, Chardonnay and Gamay Beaujolais from selected vineyards in the cool growing regions of southern Napa Valley. The Johannisberg Riesling and Chardonnay are 100 percent varietal, unblended wines. The Cabernet is softened by addition of some Merlot, as the Merlot may be strengthened by adding Cabernet, according to the needs of the wines of different vintages. The Gamay Beaujolais blends Gamay, for its youthful freshness, with Pinot Noir for its depth of fruit. With any blending, the goal is to enhance the native character of the varietal wine. Stag's Leap aims for a balanced elegance in both red and white wines, and avoids giving dominance to wood.

Warren stresses the importance of scrupulous viticultural practices in the production of fine wine. Given excellent soils and micro-climates, there are significant variations even within a 44-acre vineyard. He adapts the character and degree of pruning, cluster thinning and other practices to the various conditions of different vintage years. Separate blocs in the Cabernet vineyard are harvested separately according to their disparate ripening times, with pauses to allow late ripening vines to reach perfection.

Stag's Leap Winery

This fabulous old estate is a part of Napa Valley's historical past. It is now the home of Stag's Leap Winery, not to be confused with Stag's Leap Wine Cellars, just up the road. It is owned by Carl and Joanne Doumani, who left the world of Los Angeles big business in 1970.

The old hotel, now their home, is a picturesque building constructed in 1888 by Horace Chase. It has two stories of cut stone; a third story of wood was pulled down during restoration, and the roofline has been turreted to look like a Medieval fortress. Inside, the rooms are spacious and high ceilinged.

The winery building is of field stone and stands near the house. It was operated as a winery by the Chase family, using the Stag's Leap label of which their present label is a reproduction. The aging cellars and stone-lined caves are being restored in 1977 and will become their winery. Meanwhile, their grapes are being crushed and fermented at a neighboring winery, to their specifications.

The estate, home of Horace and Minnie (Meisner) Chase, was purchased after their deaths by the Fred Grange family, who converted it to a hotel in 1920. During the next decades, it was the "in" spot for the flaming youth of the period to make merry. It is rumored that, in this out-of-the-way spot, bootleg liquor flowed freely, and that the row of small cabins at the rear were occupied by ladies of the night as an added attraction. However, during its heyday some prestigious names graced the register, among them the King and Queen of Portugal.

The hotel closed in 1953, and a period of neglect set in. During its years of vacancy the house was stripped of many of its original fittings; chandeliers, doors and other salable items. The Doumanis found the remains of handsome gardens, which they are gradually conquering and taking back from the wild. The site is on a knoll, and there is a swimming pool, criss-crossed with cracks, which they hope to restore with gunnite, There are wide verandas, beamed redwood ceilings and lovely redwood paneling. A couple who occupied the field-stone carriage house from 1953 to 1970, Joseph and Rose Willis, recently wrote a book about Stag's Leap Ranch, called "Biography of a Manor House," recalling the grandeur of the Chase regime.

Stag's Leap Winery is a corporation. Carl Doumani is the president, and they have three stockholders: Lionel Banks, Bob Christen and Manuel Barboza.

The planned output at Stags Leap Winery is 10,-000 cases annually, a small operation devoted to making wine from their own 100 acre vineyard, which is gradually being replanted in Chenin Blanc, Petite Sirah, Cabernet Sauvignon and Pinot Noir.

The Herculean labor of restoring the buildings and grounds looms ahead of the Doumanis, but they are confident that it is within their capabilities, and look forward to the time when Stag's Leap Winery will assume its rightful place among valley wineries.

Domaine Chandon

After four years of development, Domaine Chandon opened in April 1977 to offer its first sparkling wines, winery tour, restaurant, and Champagne mini-museum for public enjoyment. The 100,000 case per year winery was designed to reflect both Napa Valley and Champagne winery features, particularly the native stone walls and arched entries. The buildings are barely visible from Highway 29, and leave a clear view of the Mayacamas mountains for Domaine Chandon's neighbor to the east, the City of Yountville.

The sparkling wines which are the principal products of Domaine Chandon reveal their heritage: the Napa Valley winery has nearly unlimited access to the resources of its French parent company, whose subsidiaries also include the prestigious champagne houses of Moet & Chandon, Ruinart and Mercier as well as Hennessy cognac and Dior perfumes.

Under the expert guidance of Moet's chef de caves, M. Edmond Maudiere, Domaine Chandon has applied the traditional methode champenoise to the creation of its sparkling wines: Chandon Napa Valley Brut and Chandon Cuvee de Pinot Noir. The carefully considered balance of these cuvees result from M. Maudiere's twenty-five years as a master blender.

Chandon Napa Valley Brut and Chandon Cuvee de Pinot Noir differ only in the composition of their cuvees, the blending of which can be considered the most demanding process of the methode champenoise. For the Napa Valley Brut, M. Maudiere blended Pinot Noir and Chardonnay grapes in a 2:1 proportion to create a traditional champagne-style sparkling wine. The Cuvee de Pinot Noir is a fuller-bodied sparkling wine made entirely from Pinot Noir grapes; this cuvee is a blend of Pinot Noirs from several different locations in the Napa Valley, notably the cooler Carneros region.

In order to control the winemaking process from start to finish, Domaine Chandon owns 900 planted or plantable acres of vineyard land in the Napa Valley. The biggest plot is the 600-acre Carneros ranch, part of which spills over the county line into Sonoma. This viticultural region attracted the attention of Domaine Chandon's president, John Wright, when the company was first established because its climate and growing conditions resemble those of Champagne.

To add other dimensions to its cuvees, Domaine Chandon owns a 200-acre vineyard on Mt. Veeder and a 130-acre vineyard surrounding the winery west of Yountville. Blending grapes of various areas of origin, different vintages, and several varieties gives the cuvees the desired complexity and allows a skillful blender to maintain a definite style from year to year despite annual variation in harvest quality.

Visitors are welcome to Domaine Chandon. Upon arrival visitors may enjoy a collection of antique vineyard and winery tools from Champagne, including two large 19th century presses, prior to departing on a guided tour of the winery.

The winery and restaurant are closed to the public Tuesday and Wednesdays.

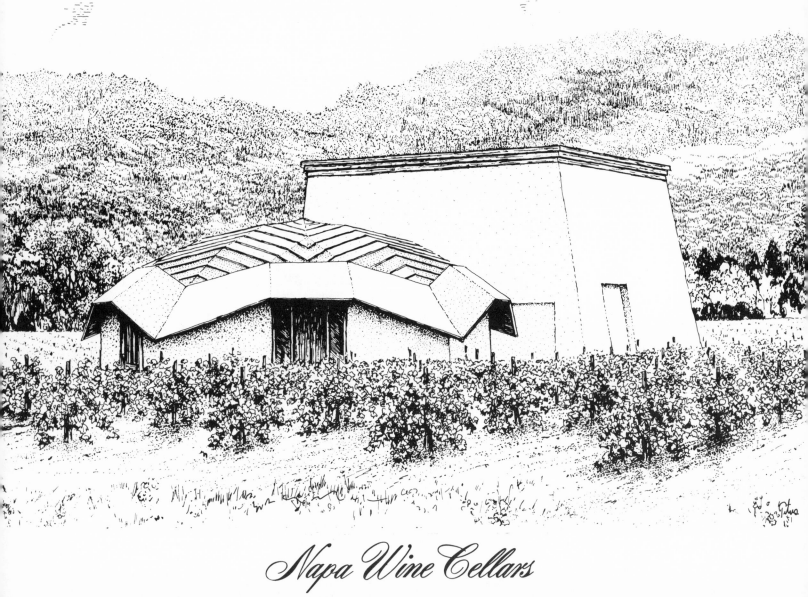

Napa Wine Cellars

NAPA WINE
CELLARS

1972
Napa Valley

Chardonnay

PRODUCED & BOTTLED BY
NAPA WINE CELLARS • OAKVILLE, CALIFORNIA
ALCOHOL 12% BY VOLUME

This new winery is already becoming a valley landmark because of its unusual design and structure. It is located one mile north of Yountville, on the west side of Highway 29, and is owned and operated by Charles Woods of Napa.

The winery, opened recently to the public after being under construction for the past two years, is composed of a geodesic dome in the front, with a truncated pyramid-shaped structure at the rear.

In the dome section, 50-gallon oak cooperage is stacked along the curving sides, with larger wooden barrels toward the center. This is the bulk storage section. There is a sales counter at the front of the room, where patrons may buy the wines.

The dome room is highlighted by a skylight of stained glass depicting grapes and leaves in their natural colors of amber, wine and green. Patrons are charmed with the intimate setting, surrounded by the sleeping wines.

Charlie Woods is his own winemaker, a business that grew out of a hobby, as with many others. What makes his story unusual is that he is a former resident of Montana, a state not noted for wine growing or wine making. He had a winemaking grandfather in France, however, and while his early years were spent in construction and engineering, he experimented with making his own wines.

In 1972 he sold his business interests, came to Cali-fornia and bought a 43-foot sailing boat, on which he and his wife Barbara ambitiously hoped to make a trip around the world. They got as far as Mexico; then, as it was getting late in the season, temporarily abandoned the scheme to winter over in San Francisco. Being an amateur winemaker, Woods made frequent visits to Napa Valley. This resulted, in a few months, in Charlie selling his boat and buying a piece of highway property, including some three acres of bearing Chardonnay vines. He was ready to launch his building operation.

To the often-asked question, "Why the dome?" Charlie replies that he had always wanted to engineer and build one because of the challenges it respresented. It is an entirely new technology, he explains, and the most efficient structure obtainable, in terms of use of space.

The rear of the building, the 27-foot pyramid-shaped structure, is the fermenting room, with separate compartments for red and white wines. This building also contains case storage. The connecting room is the bottling area. The first crush was in 1975, with the operations with one assistant.

Woods is a soft-spoken young man who is proud of his French winemaking heritage, and believes devoutly in the future of his small, quality winery, his ability to achieve the excellence he desires in his wines, and believes there will be no problem in selling the 5,000 to 10,000 cases annually which he envisions as his top production. He plans selective buying of hillside-grown grapes, he says, those with low per-acre yield, to achieve maximum flavor and character.

Villa Mt. Eden

Mt. Eden is the placid peak just north of the Oakville Crossroads that picturesquely blends into the Napa Valley at the Silverado Trail. At its base we find Villa Mt. Eden, a vine growing and wine-making operation that has nearly a hundred years of history. Vineyards were first planted on the site now occupied by Villa Mt. Eden Winery in the year 1881, according to the *History of Napa & Lake Counties* published that same year in San Francisco. The 1880's saw the real birth of Napa Valley as a wine producing region although grape growing dates back well into the 1850's and 1860's when Charles Krug and other pioneers settled here.

The St. Helena Star reported in September, 1887: "The Mt. Eden Vineyards owned by G. S. Meyers, and lying east of Rutherford, consist of 108 acres, and are this year yielding a fine crop. They are rented by J. B. Elliot and Henry Meyers who are making up the crop in the commodious cellar belonging to the fine estate." Zinfandel and Riesling were probably among the first varieties planted by Meyers in 1881. Not far from Villa Mt. Eden there lives a 93-year-old gentleman who can recall picking grapes and making wine for George Meyers. He recalls the sale of the winery in 1913 to Nick Fagiani. Fagiani sold the ranch to Schenley Distillery who owned the property until 1946 when they sold to Constantine Ramsey. Ramsey operated the ranch for 24 years when he sold to the McWilliams.

Today as you drive through the stone pillars down the road to the main house, stables, and winery, a certain order and neatness indicates a well managed ranch. Since 1970 James and Anne McWilliams have owned the property. Jim is involved in the world of finance and Anne is a former Giannini. They share a true interest in wine and have considerably upgraded their ranch with new plantings and the winery facility.

The ranch manager is Nils Venge, from the wine importing family. He displays boundless energy in his position, which includes being the winemaker as well as vineyard manager, crew boss, tractor driver, fence and barn builder and the mark of his talents can be seen everywhere. He came to the Ranch well equipped. After graduating from U.C. Davis School of Enology and Viticulture he received further training by planting 400 acres in "Los Carneros" for Krug, co-managing the Sterling vineyard operation, and making wine under Joe Heitz.

Today the vines have been planted, some bearing, some not, and the wine has been made, some has been released with great acceptance and more is yet to come. The 87 acres on the ranch that has been planted includes: Cabernet Sauvignon, Pinot Noir, Chardonnay, Merlot, Carignan (sold to another winery), Chenin Blanc, and Napa Gamay. The Gewurztraminer, also grown on the ranch, has the distinction of receiving label recognition from the Heitz Cellars release of their 1971, 1972, and 1973 vintages. The projected volume of Mt. Eden will be between 12-15,000 cases a year and this product will reflect the dedication to premium quality wine witnessed at Villa Mt. Eden Winery.

Robert Mondavi Winery

This winery, just north of Oakville on Highway 29, is a perfect example of maintaining old family tradition and wedding it to the best of the new. It was founded by Robert Mondavi, of C. Mondavi & Sons at Charles Krug, after what is described by Leon Adams as "a family tiff." Leaving his younger brother Peter in charge of Charles Krug Winery, Bob left the family firm in 1966 to begin construction on his own. Mondavi shares ownership in the enterprise with Sick's Ranier Brewing Company of Seattle.

The handsome Mission-style winery, designed by Architect Cliff May, is set back among vineyards, with long corridors, Spanish tile floors and dark wood paneling, and is dedicated to hospitality and community involvement. In this setting, Robert and his elder son Michael make up a father-and-son team which has been advantageous to both. They have established their own label and gained it a position of respect in the valley.

Although it is a large winery, one million plus gallons fermenting capacity, and has experienced several building expansions since it was founded, every effort is made to give it an aura of friendliness and informality. The Mondavi approach to wine tours and tastings involves the handling of visitors in small groups, having several small tasting rooms, and giving visitors a pleasing feeling of stature and importance. The retail sales room plays down the commercial aspect, while selling visitors

one-tenth of the winery's considerable output. Public Relations Director Margrit Biever speaks eight languages, including Japanese, and charms visitors by addressing them in their own tongue.

The winery is supplied with grapes by some 800 acres of varietal vineyards in the Oakville-Yountville area. Each piece of equipment purchased is of the finest and most modern design and manufacture, with jacketed stainless steel tanks, small European oak cooperage, and a well-equipped laboratory for its staff of enologists. The Mondavis, father and son, have combed Europe and the USA to gather together the best of equipment and technique, which is constantly being re-evaluated.

Robert Mondavi is a dynamic, slightly graying man with 38 years' experience in winemaking since his graduation from Stanford in 1936.

Bob Mondavi has to his credit many years of community service; as past president and director of Napa Valley Vintner's Association, a founder and director of Napa Valley Wine Technical Association, and as a member and former board chairman of Wine Institute. His is total involvement—if he takes a trip, it is a "busman's holiday" to visit, view and learn from other wineries in other places.

Early in his involvement with wine, Bob realized that the trend away from bulk wines to fine table wines was the direction of the future. With this in mind, he traveled extensively during the next two decades. On the East coast, he found that the image of California wines desperately needed upgrading. Whatever their merit, the wines had not achieved acceptance in the best restaurants and retail shops. Bob Mondavi threw him-

The inner courtyard at Mondavi.

self into an intensive campaign to find the reason behind this lack of prestige, and bent his considerable energies toward changing the picture.

He spent the years from 1943 to 1960 in traveling, studying, selecting, buying, tasting, evaluating and comparing California wines with those acclaimed as the world's best. Several times each year he traveled to Eastern and Mid-Western cities, an ambassador for California wines. The industry owes him a debt of gratitude for his unflagging diligence in pursuing this goal until, in the 1960's, it was finally achieved, and California wines, particularly Napa Valley wines, were accorded their place in the sun.

If no man is a hero to his valet, he is usually less so to his immediate family. However, his son Michael is one of Bob's most sincere admirers. Mike came into the business during his college years, starting at the bottom, given no special consideration because he was the son of the boss. Bob insisted that his son learn every phase of the business from the ground up. "My first job was in sanitation," remembers Mike. "That's a fancy name for scrubbing barrels." Now head of production and sales at the winery, he is well versed in every detail of the operation, and his thorough grounding has served him well.

A younger son, Tim, soon to complete his studies in enology at UC Davis, will join the family firm, where he has been working during summer vacations. He has learned all phases of the winemaking business, according to his father's theories of winery procedures.

The Robert Mondavi theories of winemaking include a firm belief in aging in wood to bring out the character and complexities of the wines. "The kiss of wood" is of vital importance, they believe, and a touch of oak is evident in all Robert Mondavi wines.

Mike believes that climate, soil, grape variety, facilities, knowledge and know-how, plus desire and will, make an unbeatable combination in producing fine wine. Of these, he believes, climate is the most important, and the climate of Napa Valley the greatest asset the Mondavi wines can claim. However, desire and will are among the strongest elements the Mondavi team has brought to the endeavor.

The wines produced have won recognition from upper echelon wine people. Eleven leading winemakers in California sampled their own Cabernet Sauvignon at a blind tasting in September, 1972. The wine writer-lecturer Robert Balzer conducted the tasting and found Robert Mondavi's 1969 Cabernet Sauvignon to be the winner.

The Vineyard Room, a large facility at the rear of the complex, opening on wide green lawns, has a rotating display of prominent Napa Valley and California artists. It is the setting for many community events.

Every Sunday in July some of the great names in the jazz music scene appear for the summer concert series at Mondavi Winery. Informal seating is on the lawn and guests can enjoy a picnic lunch and chilled wine while reclining under the warm afternoon sun.

Wine classes and symposiums, gourmet cooking classes and an occasional classical concert are held here throughout the year. In the winter the Vineyard Room is the setting for a classic film festival, with wine tasting during intermission.

Cakebread Cellars

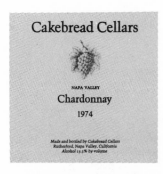

Cakebread Cellars

NAPA VALLEY
Chardonnay
1974

Made and bottled by Cakebread Cellars
Rutherford, Napa Valley, California
Alcohol 13.3% by volume

Jack and Dolores Cakebread are founders and owners of this new cellar at 8300 St. Helena Highway, St. Helena. The winery is a new building, constructed of redwood in the architecutral style of an early California barn.

The lines are pleasing, and there are two hand-carved redwood signs. All is the work of Jack Cakebread and some of his friends, working with his own design. The winery is small but adequate for the proposed production of 4000 cases of wine annually. It will be completely self contained when it is completed. An outside concrete pad is used for crushing, the ground floor for winemaking and a small laboratory, and the upper floor, reached by a well-constructed and sturdy stairway, is used for storage.

Wines produced by Cakebread Cellars are Cabernet Sauvignon, Sauvignon Blanc and Chardonnay. The 22-acre vineyard adjacent to the winery is planted to these grape varieties, a young vineyard just coming into production. Purchased grapes from the surrounding area will be used when necessary to make the wines. Cakebread is his own winemaker; he believes in using natural processes, with a minimum of fitering or fining. As production is small and will remain so, only these three wines will be made. Effort will be concentrated on making them as good as can be obtained from their own prime varietal grapes.

Cakebread is an established commercial photographer in Oakland, and he and his family are also involved in an auto repair business in the bay area. They have been engaged in agriculture in the Brentwood area for many years. His photographs have been used in a number of books, a recent one being Nate Kroman's "Treasury of American Wines," published in 1974.

The two sons of the family are interested in the wine industry; one is enrolled in the Enology Department at the University of California, Davis; the other a major in business administration.

The Cakebread approach to winemaking is casual but careful and dedicated. He is pleased with his welcome into the wine community. His gradual entrance —1977 will be his fifth vintage—has been assisted by many knowledgeable wine men involved with the industry in Napa Valley. Although the cellars are small, new and relatively unknown, such celebrated oenophiles as Harry Waugh, the British wine buff and writer, have found their way to his door.

The winery setting is rural and pleasant, back from the road at the end of a long lane. There are trees and grassy slopes, a lake, with birds and wildflowers in spring. An old vineyard and cow pasture occupied the site until it became a vineyard planted to prime varietal grapes.

Distribution has never been a problem for Cakebread Cellars; the small amount of wine so far released has been sold as soon as it became available.

There is no tasting, and the premises may be viewed by advance appointment.

Inglenook Vineyards

NAPA VALLEY
JOHANNISBERG RIESLING
*A dry white table wine with fresh fruity flavor
and blossoming* 1974 *aroma of the
noble Johannisberg Riesling grape. Serve chilled.*
*Produced and Bottled by Inglenook Vineyards
Rutherford, California Alcohol 12% by Volume*

Captain Gustave Niebaum could have built his winery anywhere in the world. He chose Napa Valley, purchasing the property south of Rutherford in 1880. At the time he bought the estate it was a sanitarium, celebrated for its mineral springs and health-giving climate.

Gustave Ferdinand Nybom (later Niebaum) was born in 1842 under Russian rule in Helsinki, Finland. He went to sea as a boy, and through diligent enterprise, sailed a ship to Alaska under his own command in 1864. By 1867 he had become so proficient at bartering for furs and acquainting himself with the region that he became a partner in the Alaska Commercial Company, which paid the U. S. government more for the exclusive fur sealing rights than the government paid for the entire Alaska purchase.

Having accumulated a fortune, he bought the 1000-acre estate known as Inglenook, a Scottish expression meaning "cosy corner" or "fireside." Niebaum was determined to make Inglenook the most celebrated winery in California. He imported cuttings from the finest vineyards in Europe, planting them with care and regard for maintaining and enhancing the beauty of nature. Along with the fine oak cooperage he imported from Germany, he also procured an unprecedented and extremely valuable library of books dealing with wine.

To give his wines a proper home, Captain Niebaum erected the cellar and winery, completed in 1887. It was said to have no equal, for perfection of detail and elegant finish, anywhere in America. The architecture is semi-Gothic. The stone and iron structure, with its arched vaults, was a model of efficiency and cleanliness, and the Captain held his crew to a high standard in all winery operations.

Frona Eunice Wait, writing in 1889, says: " 'Mould, cobwebs and dust, did you say?' remarked the genial manager, Mr. John Armstrong, upon a recent visit to Inglenook. 'I assure you, Madam, that if Captain Niebaum should discover either . . . in any of the nooks and crannies, I should be obliged to pack my traps and get, despite the fact that I have been in his service for 20 years. Cleanliness is our watchword.' "

Mrs. Wait described Inglenook as the California equivalent of Schloss Johannisberg in Germany, or Chateau Lafite in France. In 1889 the captain achieved his goal—the Inglenook wines won quality awards for overall excellence at the Paris Exposition. They continued to do so until his death in 1908.

Captain Neibaum had a penchant for success, his life history attests to his business prowess. Much like our present day Howard Hughes, outside of his close circle of prestigious friends, he was virtually unknown to the general public. He never granted a personal interview and it appears that his many days at sea fostered the solitary habits he developed on land. Nevertheless he established an elegant winery for elegant wines which still stands as a tribute to the colorful seafarer.

The tradition of making fine vintages for love of creating superlative wine, seldom showing a profit but winning acclaim in this country and abroad, continued

Cask aging wines at Inglenook.

after the death of Niebaum. Prohibition closed the winery in 1919, but Repeal in 1933 saw it reopened, its former glory restored and its integrity intact. The Captain's widow intrusted to Carl Bundschu, of the prestigious pre-Prohibition winemaking firm of Gundlach & Bundschu, the responsibility of maintaining the reputation of the winery in its days of glory. Later this responsibility was shared with John Daniel, a grandnephew of Mrs. Neibaum, and under their direction Inglenook maintained its position of prominence by allowing, as did Capt. Niebaum, only the finest bottles to be marketed.

At Inglenook it is tempting to dwell on the romance of the past but the modern era dawned in 1964 when Daniel surprised the industry and the wine community by selling Inglenook to United Vintners, thus bringing a great family tradition to an end. He remained with the winery until his death in 1970. His impact on the wine industry and his dedication to producing prestige varietal wines, without compromise, has made him immortal.

When Inglenook, under new ownership, began expansion, plans were formulated with the preservation of the historic site and bearing vineyards in mind. The picturesque winery, which has enchanted Napa Valley visitors for nearly 100 years, will become one of a complex of four buildings. The new construction includes a monolithic barrel aging cellar directly in front of the old winery. When the complex is completed, there will be a view of the winery framed by an archway at the end of the long access drive. There is to be a courtyard, with trees, flowers and fountains, in the square formed by the buildings.

This expansion places the winery in a three million plus gallon capacity category. The vineyard holdings have been enlarged to include 1500 additional valley acres formerly owned by members of Allied Grape Growers Cooperative, of which United Vintners is the marketing arm. Heublein Inc. bought United Vintners in 1968.

The same estate bottled, vintage dated varietals are still being made, as are the special "cask selection" vintages of some of Inglenook's most prestigious wines. Included is the famous Charbono, brought to the Napa Valley as early as 1861 from the Piedmont region in Italy, which resembles Barbera. The line has been expanded to include generic and "district" wines which are sold under the "Inglenook Vintage" label for less than the estate bottled wines, and the less expensive Navalle wines. Other additions include the Champagne and dessert wines.

Tours and tastings have been instituted under the new ownership. One of the sights is the Captain Niebaum sampling room, an exquisite gem furnished with pieces that would do credit to a museum. The interior, with its richly carved chairs, elaborate sideboard, large table with crystal drinking cups, all lit by the soft glow of light through stained glass windows, are as they were in the time of the Captain. Leon D. Adams calls it "a gustatory chapel."

The winemaker, Tom Ferrell, is one of the new breed of enologists turned out by the School of Enology at Davis. Inglenook places great hopes on his efforts in the future.

Beaulieu Vineyards

The Beaulieu Vineyards at Rutherford has enjoyed a position of immense prestige among Napa Valley wineries for three-quarters of a century.

The winery was founded at the turn of the century by Georges de Latour, a young Frenchman of no particular wealth, who arrived in California some 15 years earlier with wine on his mind. He began traveling the North Coast wine country, buying sediment and crust from wine tanks for making baking powder. But he was planning for the day when he would be a winegrower and winemaker.

Finally he had amassed enough capital to buy a wheat farm on the outskirts of Rutherford. The estate was named Beaulieu, "beautiful place" by his wife. He journeyed to France to bring back the finest cuttings for his vineyard, and opened a small winery. Later he acquired additional vineyards at Oakville and the Carneros District, a total of 745 acres of prime wine-growing land planted to the best varietal grapes. He would tolerate nothing second rate—where his winery was concerned, everything must be of the finest.

Some years later he bought the Seneca Ewer winery, a small building across the highway from his home vineyard, enlarging it and making it the main cellar, thus correcting the winery's only fault, lack of space, and allowing more than one half million fifths to mature in glass before shipment to wine-lovers.

When others were forced to close down during Prohibition, de Latour's business flourished, for he built up a nation-wide market in altar wines. At Repeal, he was one of the fortunate few with well-aged wines to release.

Georges and Fernande de Latour enlarged their Victorian home, which stands at the end of a mile-long avenue of flowing plum trees with white-washed trunks, amid beautiful lawns and formal gardens. They spared no expense or effort to make Beaulieu all its name implied, the most beautiful place in the valley. The setting is a valley landmark, which is depicted on the Beaulieu label.

The de Latours were gracious hosts, and entertained many of the great of their day—presidents, ministers, ambassadors and visiting nobility. Madame de Latour, the great lady of California viticulture, was famous for her generosity. When Masson Winery burned down in 1941, she came forward with an offer of red wines although the Beaulieu supply was sparse for public demand. They traveled to France every year, and this resulted in the marriage of their daughter Helene to the Marquis de Pins.

Fernande de Latour was a grande dame of the old school; Georges a cultivated country gentleman who traveled, mingled with the great, and knew wines and the men who made them. When he had to employ a new winemaker, in 1937, he went to France with his son-in-law, seeking the right man. He found Andre Tchelistcheff, a young Russian research scientist working at the winery at the Institit National Agronomique in Paris. He brought him to Napa Valley, a fact on

Vineyards seen from Beaulieu Champagne Cellars.

which he had occasion to congratulate himself. The young Tchelistcheff, in his early 30's, was fired with ambition to make fine wine, and had the flair to do it. He came with the latest French enological and viticulture research at his fingertips.

When the new enologist first tasted the valley wines, he decided that the Cabernet Sauvignon grown here was destined for greatness. For years he urged de Latour to concentrate on making only Cabernet Sauvignon, or at most one or two other wines, but this was not considered feasable at the time. He influenced de Latour to build a special cellar, aging the wine in small oak cooperage, then in the bottle, for a total of four years. The resulting wine was a sensation; Cabernet is still one of the wines for which Beaulieu is famous, and there has never been enough to satisfy the demand.

Tschelistcheff's work at Beaulieu, his influence on the image of Napa Valley wine, has probably not been equalled by any other figure in the wine world today. He made wines in the great European tradition, watching over vineyards and grapes with great devotion, harvesting at exactly the right moment. He has an uncanny ability to judge and evaluate grapes and wine, and to give each the treatment to bring out its optimum qualities. He served as consultant to other wineries, tutored many young enologists, encouraged other wine men to establish themselves in the valley.

Georges de Latour died in 1940. His wife succeeded him as head of Beaulieu until her death in 1951, when it came into possession of their daughter, Marquise de Pins.

In 1969 a family tradition came to an end when the historic winery, whose name was synonymous with the finest vintages, was sold to Heublein Inc. The estate, with its gardens, its avenue of flowering plum, together with a small vineyard and the original winery, remain in the family. The original winery is leased by Hublein as a champagne making facility.

Under Heubelin, limited expansion is the order of the day. New facilities enable Beaulieu to handle up to a 4,000-ton crush. Adjoining land was bought, and a 250,000 case warehouse constructed. Total annual production is 180,000 cases, and a modest increase is planned for future vintages. Wines are fermented in open tanks of stainless steel, and removed to aging cellar cooperage by a network of fibreglass lines. Current cellarmaster is Theo Rosenbrand; enologist is Thomas Selfridge. Another staff member, Maynard Monaghan, is completing twenty years of service at Beaulieu, giving a feeling of continuity to the enterprise. Three generations of the Tchelistcheff family have seen service at the winery; Andre's son Dmitri is technical director, and his grandson, Paul, is an apprentice in Champagne production.

The new owners emphasize that Beaulieu Vineyards has retained its identity through the change of ownership and that the traditions of Georges de Latour are not dead.

The visitor center at Rutherford Square is new, created to accomodate a large number of guests. There are gardens, fountains, art works, a tasting room and a theatre, where films on wine and winemaking are shown. All is done to lend emphasis to the concept that Beaulieu is the star in Heublein's crown.

Caymus Vineyards

1973
CAYMUS
VINEYARDS

Estate   Bottled

NAPA VALLEY

Cabernet Sauvignon

Produced and Bottled by
CAYMUS VINEYARDS
Rutherford, Napa Valley, California
Alcohol 12.5% by Volume

Caymus Vineyards is a project of Charles Wagner, an oldtime grower who became interested in making wine as a hobby, and eventually went commercial, in a limited way.

The winery, located at 8700 Conn Creek Road, Rutherford, was built by Charles and Lorna Wagner on the rear of their property in 1972. The ranch itself has an interesting history. Wagner purchased it in 1941 from Minnie Freyermuth, a daughter of pioneer Napa Valleyan Henry H. Harris, a grower and winemaker of the 1800's. Harris had bought the property from George Yount, the holder of the Mexican grant Rancho Caymus. The name "Caymus" is said to be that of the tribe of Indians living on the land at the time George Yount came to the valley in 1843.

Wagner himself is a hearty, outdoor man of ruddy countenance, with keen and piercing eye of a country man who looks on open space and likes what he sees. From an old Alsatian winegrowing family transplanted to Napa Valley he was not content merely to grow grapes. He wanted to see them reach their finest hour, to implement their blossoming into the best wine they were capable of becoming. Thus the winery came into being; a utility-type structure, functional to a spartan degree, and later augmented by an additional building for bottle storage.

Son Charles Jr. is now a part of the family operation, and father and son are giving themselves, heart and body, to the making of fine wine, enjoying every moment of it.

Wines made include Pinot Noir, Pinot Noir Blanc, Cabernet Sauvignon and Johannisberg Riesling. All wines are made from 100% varietal grapes. To these, Wagner is adding a Zinfandel, made from grapes purchased in Sonoma County, in the Dry Creek area, in Amador County and from the Lodi area. He is making, blending and aging a Zinfandel which he believes will be unlike any other on the market. It should prove complex and characterful, he says. He is uncertain when it will be released—"not until it is ready," he adds.

The Wagner vineyards are a model of good vineyard housekeeping. They are clean and well cared for, bearing out the idea that good wine depends on good grapes grown by correct vineyard techniques and with that something extra that loving care can provide. Wagner tends his grapes carefully, thinning them judiciously so the vines will not bear more fruit than they can mature successfully. There are about 70 acres in his home vineyard. With the exception of his Zinfandel mentioned above, all his wines are estate bottled.

He does not envision that this winery will ever be any larger than its present capacity, which is between 20,000 and 25,000 gallons. Wines are distributed through local retail outlets, and may also be bought at the winery in case lots.

There are no formal visitor facilities at Caymus, but interested friends of wine are welcomed by Charles and Lorna Wagner, and may view the premises, the winery buildings, the vineyards, and taste available wine.

Rutherford Hill Winery

This winery is located on a hillside east of Rutherford overlooking Napa Valley, with a tree-shaded picnic area for visitors and a natural setting studded with wild flowers in spring. Behind it are the foothills of the eastern range of the Mayacamas.

The company was established in 1976 by a limited partnership involving Freemark Abbey partners and other Napa Valley grape growers.

The building was designed in the architectural style of an old-time Napa Valley barn by John Marsh Davis, of Marin County and St. Helena, who is noted for his innovative ways with wood. There is heavy timbering, inside and out, and exposed wood gives the interior a look of warmth and hospitality. The exterior has weathered pleasingly to match the color of the surrounding hills in summer. The building is both spacious and functional, with beamed ceilings lending an atmosphere of strength and stability.

The winery is equipped with completely modern automated crushing and fermenting facilities of stainless steel, and there are large aging cellars for the European and American oak barrels and casks. The finished wines are bottled and corked in a sterile bottling room. Rutherford Hill intends to grow slowly to an ultimate production of 50,000 cases annually.

Grapes used in making Rutherford Hill wines are carefully selected from vineyards owned by members of the partnership and independently owned vineyards of proven quality, insuring an adequate supply of high quality grapes for winemaking.

The new owners will make a limited amount of Cabernet Sauvignon, Pinot Noir, Zinfandel, Chardonnay, Johannisberg Riesling and Gewurztraminer, according to William Jaeger, a general partner. Wines are being released in 1977 under the Rutherford Hill label. The high standards set by the owners for Freemark Abbey wines will be continued at Rutherford Hill.

Phillip Baxter, winemaker, and his skilled and energetic cellars crew have produced very fine and distinctive vintages for a number of years and the traditions will be continued with Rutherford Hill. Baxter is a graduate of the Fresno State University enology program.

The access road to the winery is located on Silverado Trail, one-quarter mile north of the Hwy. 128 junction east of Rutherford. Visiting and sales hours at the winery are limited, so appointments are advised. The wines are available at selected retail shops and restaurants.

Chappellet Vineyards

Among the array of men who have fled the big business scene to make wine in Napa Valley, none is more colorful than Donn Chappellet. His winery is equally dramatic, a pyramid set into a hill in an off-the-beaten-track spot called Pritchard Hill.

The pyramid is huge, 212 feet on each side at the base, with a towering roof of rust-red steel parted by long panels of glass admitting light. At the apex is a room with one of the most breath-taking views in the valley. Far below is the blue jewel of Hennessey Lake, surrounded by hills with forests of oak, madrone and fir, and 100 acres of hillside vineyard planted to noble vines.

Donn tells of leaving the Los Angeles area and his business in the food vending industry, which had unexpectedly burgeoned to bigness. "I started out with another fellow; we never planned to be big, but pretty soon we were involved with thousands of people and thousands of headaches." He parted from this multi-million dollar business with no tears, and began the search for the ideal location to build his winery. Months of scanning and screening brought him to Pritchard Hill in 1967.

Seven years and a great deal of Donn Chappellet have gone into the creation of the vineyards, the winery and the wines, which have received wide acclaim for their excellence. He expects to have the operation firmly in the black in the forseeable future, while keeping the operation small—not exceeding a 60,000 gallon capacity. Chappellet wines, originally made from their own grapes, will soon be receiving grapes from three neighbors. Donn will farm two of the ranches, with the third being operated by a retired neighbor under his direction. This will moderately expand the present production which is marketed to a select mailing list and gone almost as soon as it is announced. Donn has added scope to his wines through distribution to make them known to a wider audience and has developed markets in over twenty states at top restaurants and wine shops.

The winery was three years in the building and is a tribute to function and design. The interior is as interesting and spectacular as it is outside. It consists of one huge room, with a small office at the front. Presses, fermenters, aging cooperage, bottling and packing facilities each occupy an assigned area. The mellowness of wood, the light filtering through glass panels, the lofty apex of the pyramid stretching above, give the same feeling of awe as a grove of mighty redwoods. Along one side are stacked the small oak barrels, where precious wines sleep and ripen until they are judged ready for the bottle.

Above the winery is the long, rambling house where Donn lives with his wife Molly and their six exuberant children. The family has blended gracefully into the life of the valley wine community.

"I wanted to be a winemaker because I knew and liked wine. I wanted to do something that would be a real challenge—that would take everything I could bring to it." Thus Donn Chappellet. He has found the reality as fulfilling as its promise.

Nichelini Vineyards

James Nichelini is the third generation of a wine-making family in the old Italian tradition. The winery was founded in 1890 by Antone Nichelini, his grandfather, who came from Switzerland near the Italian border and homesteaded the tract of land in 1884. It is eleven miles east of Rutherford on Highway 128, and is a part of the John B. Chiles grant from General Vallejo, made in 1860.

Young Antone was poor but hardworking and determined. In 1890 he built the winery with native stone held together with sand and lime, money to buy cement being lacking. The building is still strong and sound. Atop the two stone stories is a frame house where Antone and his wife Caterina raised twelve children.

He planted a vineyard and made wine; his customers were miners from the many magnesium mines in Pope and Chiles Valley, where 200 Italian immigrants lived and toiled. Wages in those days included a ration of wine, and it was Nichelini wine. Mama Caterina helped out by baking crisp Italian bread in outdoor ovens for hungry customers to eat while drinking their wine.

Wineries closed during Prohibition, but Antone saw no reason why he should not make an honest living, making and selling his wine as usual. He was finally arrested and had to close down; after Repeal his son, William, came into the business at licensee. William's son Jim started helping in the family business in 1947 becoming a partner in the winery operation with his father.

Nichelini's has a crush of about 15,000 gallons, a one-man operation with extra help during the crush. The owner believes in a simple philosophy of wine-making—a continual move forward to better grapes, better methods, better wines. He has no. desire to be bigger; winegrowing and winemaking are a way of life he has found satisfying, and the increased pressures of modern business hold no attraction for him.

Visitors are welcome at Nichelini's, and they will find much to please and interest them in meeting the proprietor and viewing an old-time Italian-Swiss winery that is truly unique. The equipment in use is the same installed nearly 100 years ago, when the winery was built, except now it is motorized. Customers may sit and sip the wines on a deck adjoining the cellar, and if he is not too busy and is in good form, Jim may play the accordion for them.

Nichelini specialties are Chenin Blanc and Sauvignon Vert, but he also makes Zinfandel, Petite Sirah, Napa Gamay and Cabernet Sauvignon. The climate of Chiles Valley, at 900 feet elevation, has become interesting to other vintners, and more vineyards have been planted there. The Louis Martini Winery has planted extensive acreage north of Nichelini's, finding it to be a "low Region II." The wines of this area have a discernibly different and interesting local character.

No change seems imminent at Nichelini's, and Jim is hopeful that his son will make the winery a career as well.

Franciscan Vineyards

This redwood-faced winery, founded in 1971, is on Galleron Road one mile north of Rutherford crossroads. It has gone through several ownerships in its short life, which culminated in its sale in 1975 to Raymond Duncan of Colorado and Justin Meyer of Napa Valley. The new owners have launched the operation afresh, with some new ideas in winemaking and wine merchandising.

Duncan and Meyer took over 30,000 cases of bottled wine and 265,000 gallons in bulk, of which they immediately sold the bottled wine and part of the bulk, retaining for later release those wines which showed the most promise.

The winery, just off Highway 29, contains 22,000 square feet, adequate, Meyer estimates, for their first three years of production. Cooperage for 300,000 gallons of wine storage includes large and small oak and stainless steel.

The four to five thousand tons of grapes produced by nearly 1000 acres of vineyard owned by the partnership are largely committed for the next few years, leaving about 350 tons for the 1975 crush. With more grapes available each year, the plant should be at capacity —1500 tons—by the end of 1978. Expansion will then be considered.

One of the innovations of the new owners was the upgrading of the tasting room, where the public is invited to sample the wines. This is the best way, the owners believe, to let patrons know just what the Franciscan wines are like, as they taste the winery's product before buying.

Varietals produced by the winery are Chardonnay, White Riesling, Chenin Blanc, Muscat Canelli, Chablis, Cabernet Sauvignon, Pinot Noir, Gamay, Zinfandel, Burgundy, and the California University at Davis hybrid, Carnelian.

Meyer has a background of 10 years' winemaking experience in the valley; he is a graduate of UC Davis with a Master's degree in Enology. As winemaker, he is assistd by Leonard Berg, another Davis-trained enologist.

Leonard Berg is a nephew of Dr. Harold Berg, of the Department of Viticulture and Enology at the University of California, Davis. Dr. Berg was honored by the American Society of Enologists in 1973.

The firm has released its first bottlings, as distinguished from those on hand when they took over the winery, and is pleased with consumer reaction.

Wine sales at the winery were the order of the day in the beginning, says Meyer. After Franciscan sold off the inherited inventory, they began distributing through normal retail wine store outlets.

Duncan and Meyer are involved with another Napa Valley winery, Silveroak Cellars, launched in 1972. The sole product at Silveroak is Cabernet Sauvignon. It is planned that the two operations will be entirely separate. Silver Oak wines are also available at the Franciscan Winery premises.

Raymond Vineyards

This new winery was established in 1974 by Roy Raymond and his sons, Roy Jr. and Walter. His wife, Martha Jane, is a member of the Beringer family, a great granddaughter of Jacob, one of the founders. All of the Raymonds formerly worked at Beringer's until its sale in 1970.

When the winery was sold to the Nestle Company, the Raymonds began plans for their own winery. They purchased the property at 849 Zinfandel Lane, St. Helena, with its 90 acres of vineyard, and planned a 25,000 square foot winery building. This has not been constructed as yet because of delays in site preparation.

Meanwhile the winemaking equipment, bottling and storage facilities are housed in a large utility building near the winery site, completely insulated and air conditioned. The Raymond homes are located on the vineyard premises.

The entire setup makes a pleasant place for a family winery and the family life that goes on around it to function effectively. There are safe, spacious places for growing children to play, and while the winery and homes are completely private, they are also very much a part of the community, to which the Raymonds are bound by many ties of kindred and congeniality.

The vineyards were replanted in 1971 to Cabernet Sauvignon, Merlot, Zinfandel, Pinot Noir, Gamay, Pinot Chardonnay, Johannisberg Riesling and Chenin Blanc. From these grapes all of the Raymond wines, vintage dated and estate bottled, are made. Annual production is 5,000 cases at present with a peak of 20,000 cases when the winery is in full production.

The vineyards are a masterpiece of good vineyard practice and management techniques. Some are cordon pruned, some are trellised, according to the growth habits of the vines. Prunings are left on the ground, where they are later run through a chopper and disced into the soil. Deep wells on the place furnish water for irrigating the new vineyards and maintaining frost control.

Even in their temporary winery quarters there is evidence of the careful and efficient use of equipmnt and space that characterizes men who are doing what they most like to do, and know exactly how to go about it. Nothing is being left to chance; all is planned in detail many months in advance of developing each part of the program.

Both the younger Raymonds are educated in business administration, agriculturally oriented, and Roy Jr. has had two years of enology at UC Davis. From the beginning of the winery project, they planned to start from scratch and go all the way through the planting and establishing of a fine vineyard and winery, using all of their knowledge and expertise to make it not only a paying business, but a path to personal satisfaction and creative achievement.

This is an ideal small family enterprise, building a new tradition on the roots of an old one, and enjoying a good life along the way.

Joseph Phelps Vineyards

This is a new winery under enthusiastic ownership, with its first wine, a 1973 Johannisberg Riesling, released in the fall of 1974. The building, at 200 Taplin Road, St. Helena, is of redwood, with heavy timbering and wide overhang. The multi-level structure, with vertical siding and a cedar shingle roof, is architecturally reminiscent of an early California barn.

Its 17,000 square feet are divided into two wings, with an open area in the center, spanned by offices and administrative facilities, which tie the two wings together. The effect is pleasing, blending into surrounding foothills and vineyards.

The winery's right wing houses processing, with a bottling and aging section on the left. Offices, kitchen and laboratory are at mezzanine level. Equipment is of the finest design and manufacture, and there are many innovative ideas in practice, to insure high product quality and efficent use of time and manpower. Fermenting and holding capacity adequate for a full vintage is provided by packeted stainless steel tanks.

German oak tanks provide breakdown storage, with 3000-gallon Yugoslavian oak tanks for aging of the wines. Small cooperage of French and American oak are individually stored on steel racks for efficient removal and cleaning.

Such extreme care has been taken to preserve the environment that only one oak tree had to be removed in preparing the site. Some replanting is under way in sections where trees were cut for grazing cattle by the former owners, Connolly Hereford Ranch.

An overhead sprinkler system furnishes frost protection, and water is provided by a dam engineered to rise in a gentle slope, planted with vines to the lip of the lake, making a pleasant view of water, trees and vineyards from the winery. The Spring Valley schoolhouse, green and white with a belfry on top, a familiar Napa Valley landmark, is on the property, and has been carefully preserved, says Joseph Phelps.

The vineyard is planted to Gewurztraminer, Sauvignon Blanc, Johannisberg Riesling and Chardonnay, with reds including Cabernet Sauvignon, Zinfandel and Sirah. These comprise the estate-bottled wines, which will be about 30,000 cases annually from their own vineyards as they come into bearing. Where other grapes are used, the grower will usually be given credit.

Winemaker-ranch manager Walter Schug, a graduate of the viticulture and enology school in Geisenheim, Germany, came to the USA in 1961. He was trained in Germany, working for major premium wineries of the Rhine area. After coming to Napa Valley, he served as North Coast representative for E. & J. Gallo, in charge of grower relations and quality control.

Although a very young winery, some interesting things are afoot at Joseph Phelps. They have made a small quantity of a varietal French Syrah wine (no relation to Petite Sirah)—the only such bottling made in the USA. This is the grape, a native of upper Rhone valley, from which the famed Hermitage and Cote Rotie wines are made.

Heitz Wine Cellars

Joe Heitz has lived in California for three decades, coming first in 1944 after being stationed there during his service in the Air Force. He enrolled at Davis, and graduated with a Master's degree in viticulture and enology.

For the next decade he worked at various leading wineries, including some years at Beaulieu with Andre Tchelistcheff. He later taught viticulture and enology at Fresno State College.

In 1961, Joe and his wife Alice decided they were ready to begin their own winery. They bought the Leon Brendel "Only One" Grignolino winery south of St. Helena, along with 8 acres of Grignolino grapes. Joe still makes Grignolino, said to be the best in California.

The next years were a time of hard work, building up their winery and their label. They had great confidence in their own ability to taste and judge wines, and they selected, blended, matured, bottled and sold wines under the Heitz label. Joe had acquired a reputation for sincerity and integrity; growers with exceptional grapes liked to sell them to him, for they knew they would be handled with respect and expertise. His reputation among connoisseurs sprang up almost at once, and has continued. Alice began assembling a mailing list to be notified as wines were available.

In 1964, Joe and Alice acquired another winery and vineyard, Spring Valley Ranch, at the end of Taplin Road. It had a picturesque old winery of native cut stone, built in 1898, and Heitz equipped it with the best of winemaking machinery and cooperage—a Willmes press, stainless steel fermenters, small Limousin oak cooperage. The ranch has 160 cares of rocks, hills and old vines. Joe planted 20 acres of Grignolino grapes and expects to plant an additional 40 to 50 acres of grapes in the near future.

It is not Joe's intention to dilute his talents as a winemaker with large holdings of vines. He has developed over the years a "solid source of fine grapes from reliable growers", and this asset has helped develop the present day reputation of Heitz Cellars. Grapes from the prestigious growers have the vineyard origin printed on the label and each bottle is numbered as it is labeled.

Alice works along with her husband, while making a family home of the old farmhouse. They make a great team. She is a famous cook and he is a famous winemaker. Wine writer William Massee comments, "Joe is a superb winemaker with an exceptionally keen palate, only seen once or twice in a generation." Joe is always ready to share his knowledge with others. He has trained many young winemakers now making their own reputations. Bob Travers of Mayacamas and Mike Golick of Chateau Montelena are two men who worked with Heitz.

A new winery of cement block and timbers was built in 1972 for aging red wines, storage and offices. The original winery off Highway 29 is the Heitz Cellars tasting and sales room. The eldest Heitz son, David, a recent graduate of Fresno State University, is involved in the family winery and vineyard operation.

V. Sattui Winery

The V. Sattui Winery label is an old one, dating back to 1885. It was reactivated in 1975 by the great grandson of the founder, Daryl Sattui, who designed and built a winery at the corner of White Lane and Highway 29, two miles south of St. Helena.

The winery is an off-white stucco structure, 60 by 72 feet, of early California architecture, and set in an old walnut orchard. The interior has heavy timbering, exposed beams and massive redwood doors.

The original winery, founded by Vittorio Sattui of San Francisco, had a capacity of 150,000 gallons, and attained a reputation for quality wines at the turn of the century. With the advent of Prohibition, Vittorio toyed with the idea of bootlegging, but opted to stay on the side of the law. He went into the insurance business, which has engaged the family ever since.

Daryl had long dreamed of re-establishing the family name in the wine industry. A born entrepreneur, Daryl started his first business venture at age seven, and built and operated a number of enterprises during his school years. On graduation from high school, he cashed out his business interests and realized enough money to pay his way through college, with funds left to travel in Europe for two years. There he met his Finnish wife, Mirja.

Returning to the USA, Daryl, with the encouragement and support of his family, began the fulfillment of his lifelong ambition. His background of business management, a Master's degree in Marketing and Accounting, plus work experience at a number of other wineries, gave him confidence as he began the task of building the winery and developing the grounds.

His winemaking equipment is small scale, and includes an old-fashioned crusher, a wooden basket press, and his great grandfather's 100-year-old corker, still used to cork each bottle of Sattui wine. There are handsome 1000-gallon German oak ovals and 60-gallon French oak barrels for aging. A small tasting room occupies a corner of the winery, where visitors may view the winemaking operations as they sample.

Another section of the building holds a well-stocked cheese and gift shop, featuring a large selection of cheeses, breads, salamis and other gourmet foods. These may be bought for an al fresco picnic under spreading walnut trees, on tables made from old wine casks.

Daryl and Mirja run the business together, working long hours and making wine under the supervision of consultant Steve Bertolucci. Wines are either made at the winery or purchased from neighboring wineries and cellared at Sattui and sold at medorate prices. The wines include Zinfandel, Carbernet Sauvignon, White Riesling and Chardonnay—natural, full character wines, 100 percent varietal and vintage dated unless otherwise specified on the label. Reds are unfiltered and unfined.

The Sattuis live in a 70-year-old house on the premises. "We don't expect to see a profit for years to come," says Daryl. "We aren't looking for a fast buck, but for a satisfying way of life."

Sutter Home Winery

Sutter Home Winery was founded in 1874 by a Swiss winemaker, John Thomann. Later, in 1900, John Sutter and his brother Jacob purchased the winery and changed its name to the present title. (John Sutter is not the Sutter of Sutter's Fort, but a cousin.)

In 1946 it was purchased by the Trinchero family, John and Mario. Present owners are Mario and Mary Trinchero and their two sons, Louis (Bob) and Roger.

Under the Trincheros, the business was operated for many years as a bulk winery, making and selling wine to customers who came to the winery with their jugs to be filled. Their product was well known and popular with the Italian community, and provided them with a good living.

However, since the wine explosion in the valley, and with younger members of the family exerting their influence on policy, it was decided that they needed a specialty—some particular wine or wines that would set them apart. They came upon a Zinfandel vineyard in the Shenandoah Valley in Amador County, and from its grapes made a smallish amount of wine that proved interesting to wine palates.

Encouraged by this success, they made more the next year, and more each succeeding year until now 85 percent of the wine made at Sutter Home is Zinfandel. The balance is their line of dessert and aperitif wines. These

bottlings include a sweet and a dry Vermouth, and a Moscato Amabile.

The operation has expanded; in the past year it has increased production by 80,000 gallons, bringing the winery up to a 170,000 gallon capacity. They have installed an automatic bottling line, and their wines now have national distribution. Their Zinfandel has always been in short supply, inadequate to meet the demand for this exceptional wine.

This is truly a family winery—members of the family do all the chores, with Bob making the wine, Roger handling sales, Mario and Mary working half day at the winery, and a daughter and daughter-in-law handling tasting room, retail sales and secretarial work. They often laugh about selling good red wine, aged four or five years, for $2 a gallon, in the old, pre-wine-bust days. The present day wine, including the vintaged Zinfandel, is moderately priced for today's market. It is an unusually heavy, robust wine, well balanced, with an excellent raspberry nose. There is some tannin, which allows further aging in the purchaser's callar.

The Trincheros of Napa Valley are from a wine-making background in Asti, Northern Italy. They have no vineyards of their own, purchasing all their grapes to provide the annual sale of 20,000 cases. As with many other valley wineries, they have steadfastly refused all offers to sell. Younger members of the family, grandsons of Mario and Mary, are looking toward involvement in the family winery in the future.

There is no formal hospitality center, but visitors are welcomed, and there is always one of the family on hand to offer tasting and wine talk to interested patrons.

Louis Martini Winery

This winery was founded by Louis M. Martini, who died in 1974 at the age of 87, but lived long enough to become a legend in his own time. He was of the old school, lent infinite color and drama to the industry image, and made very fine wines over the years.

The winery, at the southern boundary of St. Helena, was built by Louis himself in 1933. It is a concrete and hollow tile insulated cellar where, for many years, visitors tasted the wines at a long counter adjacent to barrels of wine in the storage cellar, the pleasant odor of sleeping vintages in their nostrils. In recent years an addition on the north side of the building was constructed, housing a handsome tasting room and executive offices.

Louis Michael Martini was born in Pietra Ligure on the Italian Riviera in 1887. He came to America at age 13 to join his father in the fish business in pre-earthquake San Francisco. The two fishermen dreamed of making wine some day, and in 1906 started a backyard winery. They were dismayed to find the entire vintage spoiled and undrinkable. So young Louis was sent to Italy to learn how to make good wine, entering the Alba School of Enology. So great were his zeal and capacity to learn that he finished the course in one year, returning home to turn out a vintage that satisfied both father and son. The wine was marketed by selling it door to door in the Italian community of North Beach.

As time went on Louis became involved with winemaking in various parts of the state. During Prohibition he established a winery in Kingsburg where he made and distributed a grape concentrate for home use, appropriately called "Forbidden Fruit." He had faith that such an unnatural law could not last long, and at Repeal he began making and shipping bulk wines.

In 1934 he built the St. Helena plant for the production of dry wines and operated both plants until 1940, when he sold the Kingsburg plant and moved operations to Napa Valley, taking his savings of twelve years to begin quietly making and storing fine table wines. The wines released created a sensation overnight and put him among the ranks of California's top winemakers.

He acquired vineyards at St. Helena, southern Napa County and in Sonoma County. His most famous vineyard, called Monte Rosso from its red volcanic soil, is situated at 1000 feet elevation on the ridge dividing Napa and Sonoma Counties. This vineyard has produced some top quality wines, which bear the appellation "Mountain" on the label. In all, the family owns some 800 acres of prime varietal vineyards, the latest acquisition being in Chiles Valley.

He built a family home adjacent to the old stone winery where he cellared some of his first wines during the 30's.

A picture of this giant of the industry as he was in his prime is found in Dr. Angelo Pellegrini's "Americans by Choice." The senior Martini is depicted as dining robustly, drinking wines with gusto, enjoying fam-

Martini's Monte Rosso Vineyards.

ily, friends, home and work with an earthy yet urbane zest and love of life. He is shown working in the winery, exchanging with co-workers the flashes of temper that, among Italians, indicates "health, virility and love."

In appearance, Louis was a typical North Italian, fair haired and blue eyed, with broad shoulders and standing almost 6 feet tall. He prided himself on his cooking, as well as his wines, and as an octogenarian one of his favorite activities was preparing luncheon for his friends. His natural wine palate and nose, which he viewed as his greatest assets, were augmented by a lifetime—66 years—spent in their cultivation.

Although Louis M. Martini turned over the reins of the winery operation to his son Louis Peter in 1960, he maintained an office at the winery and came in every day until the last few months of his life. As is traditional in many European families, he was every inch the head of the family and business, the boss, as long as he lived.

The younger Martini is president of the firm which, in spite of its size—over two million gallons storage capacity—is still a personal one, reminiscent of the small, family-owned wineries in the valley. There is a strong family feeling among the employees, an aura of strength and continuity about the winery.

The red wines are robust and straightforward, with both character and potential. The Special Selection bottlings, available only at the winery and then in limited quantities, are very smooth and well-rounded, and carefully chosen for their potential to acquire the assets age can bring to a fine wine. Among the whites are a rare varietal Folle Blance, from the Monte Rosso vineyard, and an exceptional Gewurztraminer, a dry and spicy wine. A very delicate white wine is Moscato Amabile, sold only at the winery, slightly sweet and sometimes bubbly.

There are also generic wines, which those whose purse does not permit vintage wine on the table every day find very satisfying. The Mountain Red and Mountain White wines are good everyday wines, forceful and pleasing. The line, all sold under the Louis M. Martini label, includes some 30 table and dessert wines.

The son, Louis P. Martini, has studied enology and viticulture at University of California's Berkeley and Davis campuses. He looks, in his middle years, a great deal like his famous father, with the same big frame, height and coloring. He has the same direct, straightforward way, believing sincerely in the dignity of hard work and that the making of fine wines is not done in a day. The Martinis believe that skillfull and judicious blending is the secret of making superior wines.

The Martinis live in the old Edge Hill winery, built in 1870, its two-foot-thick walls making a comfortable dwelling. There are two daughters and two sons, all interested in the winery. Louis P. plans and hopes that the family tradition of winemaking will be carried forward in their hands for the foreseeable future.

The fiery, dynamic head of the family is gone, but his influence on the wine community lingers, and he will not be forgotten when wine men foregather and old wine stories are recalled.

Spring Mountain Vineyards

This winery was founded in 1968, using as its headquarters the basement of a century-old home just north of Christian Brothers at St. Helena. The stately Victorian mansion was built in 1876 by Fritz Rosenbaum, a San Francisco glass merchant, and called Johannaberg Vineyards.

Vineyards and buildings had fallen into disrepair, but caught the eye and imagination of Michael Robbins, a San Francisco businessman with an engineering and law background, during a business trip to the valley in 1962. He spent the next years restoring it, and assembled a winemaker's dream of a winery in its below-level basement. His first Spring Mountain wine was introduced in 1970.

By 1974, ready for expansion of his facilities, Mike bought the Tiburcio Parrot home and winery, Miravalle, located on a hillside off Spring Mountain Road. The elegant old estate crowns a little rise, and as the name implies, commands a view of the valley.

A member of a banking and finance family, Parrot believed in the valley as superlative wine country, and in hillside vineyards as growing the finest grapes. He planted his vineyards, the choicest French varieties, as high as horse and plow could go. Parrot sold many of his grapes to Beringer Winery. He also produced a very fine claret which he called "Margaux", which won honors among knowledgeable wine lovers of the day.

This handsome property was purchased from the Parrot estate by Wallace Hyde, who owned it until its sale to Robbins. The house is a larger facsimile of the Rhine House of Beringers, of whom Parrot was a friend and contemporary.

The old redwood winery building, in front of a 90 foot cave dug into the hillside, has been torn down and a new winery has been built of an architectural style akin to the house and Victorian barn.

The first Spring Mountain wines, a Chardonnay, a Cabernet Sauvignon and a Sauvignon Blanc, released in 1970, were proclaimed excellent by connoisseurs. The 1973 crush yielded 6,500 cases, and the winery output will continue to increase to reach an estimated capacity of 18,000 cases when the vines are mature. Replanting of the Miravelle vineyards will begin soon, says Mike.

Mike Robbins' devotion to detail has won him fame in his dutal professions of engineering and law. The family, including two young sons, are winery workers. His winemaker is Charles Ortman.

Both Mike and Shirley feel the valley is a great place to make fine wine because of climate and soil, and "a great tradition which motivates winemakers to achieve the highest form of the winemaker's art." The future, they believe, is very bright.

The proliferation of small wineries is an ecological as well as an economic asset, they say. It is, in the widest meaning of the words, the highest and best use of this national asset.

Chateau Chevalier

Beringer Brothers owned this gorgeous Spring Mountain vineyard until F. Chevalier purchased the property in 1884. The winery, described by Leon D. Adams as "one of the loveliest old stone cellars in the country" in his recent book, "The Wines of America," was built in 1891.

It was given to Chevalier's son George, with the elder Chevalier personally attending to all of the winery operations. He won acclaim for his wines, distributed throughout the nation, by 1889. The industry was well aware of his superior products, which included "Castle" brand wines, clarets and brandies. He maintained offices on North Main Street in Los Angeles, with headquarters on Washington Street in San Francisco.

The next major owners were Howard Hart and his family, long-time residents of the valley, who owned it from 1915 to 1940. Mr. and Mrs. Leslie Rogers maintained the estate for the next 22 years, lavishing love and care on the building and grounds. The wine market at that time did not warrant the restoration of the vineyards, but the formal gardens on the estate were brought back to a gracious splendor.

Rogers died in 1960, and Chateau Chevalier was purchased by a trio of investors, called "Chateau Chevalier Associates," in 1962. Their infrequent visits to the estate launched it into a period of neglect and disrepair; gardens returned to the wild state and the stone steps leading to the terraced vineyards became overgrown with weeds.

Happily the present owners, Gregory Bissonette and Peter Hauschildt, purchased the Chateau in 1969, and brought new vigor and excitement to restoration of the handsome estate. Under their ownership, the 10,000 case winery made its first crush in 1973. The estate grown wine will be labeled Chateau Chevalier and will be a Cabernet Sauvignon and Chardonnay. A secondary label, Mountainside Vineyards, will be a product reflecting the Chateau ability to select and buy grapes with an eye towards moderately priced wine.

Their enthusiasm in reclaiming the abandoned vineyard and grounds was apparent on a recent visit to the famous Chateau. Gregory was driving the tractor down a row of terraced vines, with his young son, Gregory Jr., on his lap. Following the tractor was his wife Kathy and a Mexican helper. They were hurrying, just ahead of a winter rain, to abate future weed problems. It was an inspiring sight—a united young family working toward a worthy goal.

After tasting the wines at the Chateau, one can feel assured that the style and tradition of a family-owned and operated winery will continue to be reflected in the wines. The Bissonettes, who co-occupy the stone building along with the wines, are a large family—there are six children—and their intention is to make fine wine.

There is an aura about the place and the people that will please and inspire any visitor to the Chateau. A lapsed tradition has been revitalized, and will remain vigorous and growing for years to come.

Yverdon Vineyards

A long, narrow and stony road leads to this mountain winery in a wooded section on Spring Mountain near St. Helena. The owner, Fred J. Aves, with his son Russell, bought a 50-year old hillside vineyard in 1970, cleared the land which had grown up to firs and scrub oak, and planted 10 acres of new vines. They also have 80 acres of vines on Bennett Lane in Calistoga, called Rancho Alto.

The elevation is 2,000 feet. At the end of the road is the handsome cut stone winery, made by the hands of Fred and Russell Aves and helpers. They are making and marketing their first wines while building the winery and Fred's home, with their first crush in 1971.

Aves is a former Los Angeles business man, a manufacturer of auto supplies, and his son began his business career as a mechanic and builder of racing cars. From this incongruous background they turned to an interest in wine. Fred began making it in his home, with Southern California grapes, which he soon found did not meet his expectations. He began buying Napa Valley grapes and transporting them to Los Angeles to make his wine. This led to purchase of the Rancho Alto vineyard, which in turn led to selling out the Los Angeles holdings and moving the operation to Napa Valley.

The labor involved has been prodigious, cutting and laying each stone by hand. The winery is a castle-like structure in the old school of valley winery architecture, with Tudor arches, quatrefoil stained glass windows and similar features. The stone used is a hard grade engineer stone, from which many valley wineries were made in the 19th century. They are constructing hillside tunnels for aging the wines, an anacronistic procedure not followed by wineries built during the 20th century. Tunnel construction has been complicated by the necessity for shoring up the tunnel with concrete arches as they go.

Also under construction on the winery site is Fred's home, of cut stone, a two story structure with a mansard roof. Both the winery and the home were designed by Fred, without benefit of architect, along the lines of buildings he had admired in France.

The venture has been family-contained, with the exception of a laborer or two to help with rough work. Father and son have enjoyed and taken pride in creating something uniquely their own, with their own heads and hands. All hands fall to and work at the winery when the wines are ready—Fred, his son, Russell's wife Leona, and their two young sons and daughter. It is a life style all enjoy and accept with enthusiasm.

Fred is a man of parts; besides being able to design and create intricate buildings and make wine, he is also a super gourmet cook,—"Isn't everyone?" he asks, with no idea that the answer is, sadly, "No." He cooks as naturally as he makes wine, with no feeling that he is doing anything extraordinory. The only difficulty, he says, is geeting some of the needed ingredients for a favorite dish.

The winery has a capacity of 50,000 gallons, which they plan to bring to a 100,000 gallon level within a year or two.

Ritchie Creek Vineyards

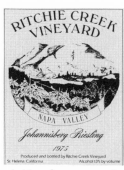

A narrow road winds up the steep incline of Spring Mountain, passing along the way some of California's most prestigious vineyards. At the very top of the two thousand foot climb, surrounded by conifer studded slopes is Ritchie Creek Vineyard. The tiny mountain estate is blessed with one of Napa Valley's most majestic views; steeply terraced hillsides stand against a backdrop of craggy mountain peaks stretching from Calistoga to St. Helena.

Ritchie Creek Winery officially had its beginnings in 1967 when Peter Minor purchased property high in the Mayacamas Mountains. He started clearing the land and planting vines that year. The four acres of vineyards are devoted entirely to Bordeaux varieties, mostly Cabernet Sauvignon and fifteen percent Merlot. Peter chose this location above all others because he felt the thin rocky soil, high altitude and northern exposure would most closely approximate the growing conditions of the French Bordeaux region. The yields from the highly stressed vines seldom reach one and a half tons to the acre, producing juice that is the essence of the variety. As berries reach maturity, every vine must be covered with plastic netting to avoid devastation by birds.

Peter was still a practicing dentist in Berkeley in 1968 when he laid the foundation for his home in the mountains. Working weekends and holidays for three years, he singlehandedly constructed a solid stone house, gathering the native rocks and mortaring them into place, the foot-thick walls took shape. Large arched doorways and windows were fitted and leaded by hand. The roof of ancient barn wood was applied over telephone pole beams. When the monumental task was complete, Peter left his practice and with the invaluable assistance of his wife, Maggie' began work on the winery.

At a tree studded site below the vineyards a hill was hollowed out, the concrete winery was constructed and the earth replaced over the top, providing natural temperature control. All that is visible is an arched doorway into the hill. The tiny five hundred square foot winery houses several years' production and a small laboratory.

In 1974 the first Cabernet Sauvignon wine was produced from the vineyard. The wine is totally unfined and unfiltered, using only traditional French winemaking techniques, with wines aged in Never Oak two years and at least two years in the bottle before release, perhaps in 1978. The result is an incredibly rich, dark and concentrated wine which will last and hopefully improve for decades.

In addition, the minors purchased a limited supply of grapes from their neighbors to produce both a White Riesling, and a Chardonnay. Their first wine, a Johannisberg Riesling, was released in 1977. Because of an extremely limited supply (eventual annual production of 700 cases) most of the wine will be marketed directly to consumers via Ritchie Creek's mailing list. Interested buyers are prompted to contact the Minors far in advance.

Beringer Vineyards

Beringer
Traubengold
A MEDIUM DRY CALIFORNIA RIESLING

Produced and bottled by
Beringer Vineyards, St. Helena, Napa Valley, California
Alcohol 12½% by Volume

The Beringer story begins in the mid-1800's with Frederick and Jacob, members of a winemaking family from Mainz on the Rhine. The lure of French winemaking techniques brought them to the Medoc, and later, in 1870, Jacob met Frederick in New York to help in his established wine marketing business.

Although all went well with the brothers, they hungered for a vineyard and winery of their own. In a visit to St. Helena, some years later, Jacob found what he sought—just the location for winery and vineyard. Here was the ideal climate—warm, with sandy soil, soft sunshine, gentle rains, and at the end of the season, brisk winter weather that gave, he felt, exactly the right conditions for the growing of quality grapes.

He found the perfect spot to erect a winery, a hillside of soft stone, which formed the ideal environment for the aging of the fine wines he planned to produce from his hillside vineyards.

In 1876 the brothers combined their talents and established the Beringer Brothers Winery. While the vineyards were being established and cellars constructed, Jacob was working at the Charles Krug Winery just down the road. Frederick built the Rhine House, a stately 17-room mansion with carved oak panels and slate roof which duplicated, as nearly as obtainable materials would allow, the old family castle on the Rhine. It remains today as a tourist attraction, as well as a tribute to Los Hermanos, The Brothers, whose desire was to produce fine wine.

The original winery was 40 by 104 feet, with walls of massive stone, and the ground floor slightly pitched to allow for drainage. Behind this three-story structure were tunnels carved into the volcanic stone hill. The Chinese provided the labor. Employing picks, shovels and sweat to remove segments of the stone, they carried out the rubble in small woven baskets, finally completing a thousand feet of tunnel.

The second story was built like the deck of a ship and caulked regularly. It was water tight, and could be flooded to a depth of several inches without a leak. The third floor was used for the crushing of grapes, employing the old technique of gravity flow during winery operations.

Horse-drawn wagons laden with grapes were led around a road at the rear of the winery to deliver their load to the crusher. The St. Helena Star reported in 1883: "The wine cellar of Beringer Bros. is large and substantial, and the most handsomely finished of any in the Napa Valley. For solidarity of build and completeness of appointments, it can have no superior anywhere. The monogram of the owners, B. B., is neatly cut in the keystone."

With the buildings completed and vineyards producing, the brothers set out to achieve their reputation for quality wine. Before Prohibition, awards were won in San Francisco in 1887; Paris in 1889 and 1900; Dublin in 1892 and Chicago in 1893.

The fame of Beringer Bros. wines and brandy continued for many years. In 1914 the survivors of the

Oak barrels in Beringer's stone caves.

two brothers' families incorporated Beringer Bros. Several women of the family became officers of the corporation. Bertha was president; Martha vice president; and Agnes Beringer Young, assistant secretary. Los Hermanos might properly have changed its name to Las Hermanas under their direction.

The name "Los Hermanos" was given the estate by a close friend, Senor Tiburcio Parrot, a Spanish gentleman of the old school, who lived in a beautiful villa above the Rhine House. They had a team of magnificent matched horses, as did the Beringers, and Miss Bertha Beringer, who wrote a history of the winery, recalls: "the elegant carriage, the sprinted team driven by a resplendent coachman in livery, in which Don Tiburcio and his lovely wife used to dash up the winding drive to call at the Rhine House."

Sr. Parrot's villa, called "Miravalle," is a replica, but on a larger scale, of the Beringer residence. The two families vied with one another in setting the pace for elegant appointments and gracious living.

For almost 100 years the winery was continously owned and operated by members of the Beringer family, and the title of "Napa Valley's oldest winegrowing family" can be accorded them. Since 1879 they produced every vintage, without exception. During Prohibition, they supplied, and continue to supply, altar and medicinal wines for the clergy and medical professions throughout the country.

Young Fred Beringer, the fourth generation of the family, today owns and operates the Bottle Shop in St. Helena, and thus continues the family's traditional association with wine.

In 1970 the Beringer family sold the winery and 700 acres of vineyard to Nestle, Inc., the Swiss-based international food company.

The Rhine House, once the center of gracious living for the Beringer family, has been fully restored to its rightful elegance. It serves as a hospitality center, so that all visitors to Beringer may view its splendors as a part of their wine tour.

Beringer is one of the most interesting valley wineries to visit because of the maze of stone tunnels cut a thousand feet into the hill behind the winery by picks of Chinese laborers. There are many beautiful wooden casks, hand carved with designs of a California grizzly, clusters of grapes and similar motifs.

Vineyards have been expanded to include 3,000 acres of vines either leased or owned in Napa, Knights and Alexander valleys. A new expansion of facilities was completed in 1975 across the road (Highway 29). Since its acquisition by Nestle, no expense has been spared to upgrade the winery and holdings to a sound commercial basis.

The winemaster at Beringer's is the highly regarded Myron Nightingale, who was a classmate at Berkeley of Louis P. Martini. He is said by William Massee to be "a legendary winemaker," having guided the destinies of Cresta Blanca and developed its famed Premier Semillon. Stephen O'Donnell is his assistant. Nightingale is busy perfecting techniques that will insure that Beringer grapes produce traditional wines of highest quality, which they must now do in quantities large enough for national distribution.

Christian Brothers Winery

A world-reknown valley landmark is Greystone Cellars. It is approached through the "archway of the elms" just north of St. Helena, and is one of the homes of Christian Brothers wines. Two other facilities, one at Mont LaSalle, the other south of the town, are a part of the complex.

Christian Brothers is an order of the Roman Catholic Church, a group of laymen whose members live in community, take vows of poverty, chastity and obedience, and give their lives to serving others. The Brothers are dedicated to education of the young, with some thirteen secondary schools and colleges supported by Christian Brothers winemaking programs.

Greystone has an interesting history, and has played a major part in creating the valley wine empire. It was built in 1889 by William Bourn, a wealthy vineyard owner, who is still remembered in the valley for his generosity and community spirit. At the time it was built, Greystone was the largest stone winery in the world. The cost, fantastic for the time, was $2 million.

Bourn was owner of two Napa Valley vineyards, of San Francisco's Spring Valley Water Company, and had extensive mining interests. He conceived the idea of establishing a growers' cooperative, to make wine from the valley grapes, age it at Greystone, and lend growers the money, ten cents per gallon, to keep afloat until their wines could be matured and marketed. But un-fortunately, this altruistic scheme came into being just as phylloxera got a foothold in the vineyards, and production of wine fell sharply.

Greystone had a procession of owners for the next fifty years. It was owned by Charles Carpy, Bisceglia Brothers, the California Wine Association, Central California Wineries, Cresta Blanca, and Roma Cellars. It was sold to Bisceglia during the Depression for an unbelievable $10,000—a building of three stories, measuring 400 by 78 feet, with a 20 by 50 foot projection at the front—a total floor space of just under three acres.

Exterior walls are hand-cut native sandstone, creating a structure of massiveness and beauty. There are Roman arches, high vaulted ceilings, huge doors and mahogany paneling. The aging facilities include imported white oak tanks of huge size, built on the site during construction of the winery. On the third floor, Champagne is produced by the Charmat method.

In 1945, the Christian Brothers, whose winery was at Martinez, leased cellar space from the owners, Roma Cellars, and in 1950 they purchased the winery outright, and moved their operation to the Napa Valley.

In the wooded hills above the valley is Mont La-Salle, an old stone winery built in 1903 by a German winemaker, Theodore Gier. The setting is one of exceptional beauty and charm, with vineyards marching up the hill, which is crowned by the handsome school and winery buildings. Here, between matins and vespers, wines are made, novices trained and visitors received. The gardens are spacious and picturesque, and the chanting in the chapel adds to a stroll among the flowers.

The winery's administrative offices are at the Mont

Mont La Salle Novitiate amidst 200 acres of vines.

La Salle location. In the lobby of the buildings are several handsome wood carvings of vineyard scenes. In one, a cowled and habited Brother is seen crushing grapes in a horse trough with a wooden club.

There is another new facility just south of St. Helena, a tribute to the far-sighted policies and shrewd business acumen of the Order. Forseeing the wine explosion in its infancy, the new complex was begun in 1965 with a warehouse which became inadequate for their expanded needs by the time it was completed. The Brothers determined to "think bigger," and made this structure the first unit of a five-phase building program. The plan is a daisy pattern, with buildings raying out from a circular center. Further segments of the expansion include buildings to house laboratories, tasting and sales rooms, warehouse space, bottling facilities, administrative offices and a large area for holding special events. Everything is designed to make, age and ship wine as efficiently as possible, with all winemaking processes fully automated.

Cellarmaster is Brother Timothy, one of the industry's most colorful figures. He has been with the Order for 46 years, involved with wines since 1935. He knows the wine business thoroughly, from planting the vine to writing the label, and has done both.

Brother Tim's internationally famous collection of corkscrews has a representative display at Greystone, along with early day presses and other winemaking equipment. He is perhaps one of the most interviewed and photographed men in the wine world, and is never too busy to talk about the Order or the wines.

His winemaking theories differ from some other valley wineries, in that his talents are directed to making the end product as uniform as possible, from year to year. The genial Brother Tim has a famous palate, and wines are blended, from two or three vintages, to produce as perfect a wine, with identifiable varietal characteristics, as can be done. Blending is always done with an eye to quality, and the result is that a bottle of any Christian Brothers wine will be the same dependable quality, year in and year out. All wines are moderately priced.

The Christian Brothers operation is the largest in Napa Valley, in point of physical size as well as production-wise, with a capacity of three and one-half million gallons of table and sacramental wines. Over 200,000 visitors pass the famous Greystone portals every year. Visitor facilities are maintained at both Greystone and Mont LaSalle, and tours and visits are eminently worthwhile.

Christian Brothers wines, Champagnes and brandies are marketed through the firm of Fromm & Sichel. The Wine Museum in San Francisco is a joint effort of the Brothers and their marketing firm, and is a mecca for visitors from the world wine scene. Gathered together there are many treasures depicting various phases of wine and wine art, handsomely housed and beautifully displayed. The Museum is a must on the agenda of all wine country visitors.

The wines produced by Christian Brothers comprise a full line of varietal and generic types, as well as Vermouth, brandy and Champagne. Their vineyards cover about 1000 acres in Napa Valley, and another 1000 acres in the San Joaquin Valley.

St. Clement Vineyards

St. Clement Vineyards, 2867 N. St. Helena Highway, is the former Spring Mountain Winery. The first Spring Mountain wines were laid down there and released in 1970. Present owners are William and Alexandra Casey.

The winery is situated in the cellars of a restored Victorian mansion capping the top of a rise, with waves of vineyard lapping at its feet. The house was built by Fritz Rosenbaum of San Francisco in 1876, and celebrated its centennial along with the nation's bicentennial.

The Caseys, frequent visitors to Napa Valley in the past, admired the hillside estate with its handsome home and well kept grounds. Inquiry at a local shop revealed that it was for sale. They could not resist buying it, says Dr. Casey, for they felt this golden opportunity might never come again. They had planned to establish a winery later, but circumstances seemed to indicate that this was the right time. They bought it in 1976, along with the equipment and some wine in the making.

Dr. Casey, a San Francisco ophthalmologist, commutes to his practice and works at the winery weekends and when he can spare the time. His young winemaker, Jon Axhelm, was formerly assistant winemaker at Spring Mountain. Dr. Casey and Axhelm rely on the guidance and expertise of Brad Webb and Robert Stemmler, wine consultants, as the new winery is launched.

The name St. Clement, pronounced with the accent on the first syllable, dates back into Casey family history, when Dr. Casey's forbears landed on St. Clement Island in Maryland.

His interest in wine goes back to a family vineyard in the East. Both Caseys are wine buffs, gourmet cooks, and enjoyers of valley wine community life. It is Dr. Casey's desire to make outstanding wine from his prime quality grapes, which he feels are worthy of the best of the winemaker's art. He released his first wine, a 1975 Chardonnay, in 1976. This wine, and a 1975 Cabernet Sauvignon, were crushed and fermented by Mike Robbins, cellared and bottled by the Caseys. The Cabernet Sauvignon will go on sale after a longer aging period.

Dr. Casey is proudest of his 1976 wines, for they are of his own crushings and fermenting. Both the Chardonnay and Cabernet Sauvignon of the 1976 vintage show great promise, he believes. The year 1976 will be remembered as a dry, warm year, and it has been expected by vintners that the grapes, with less moisture and more warmth than usual, would produce some very interesting and characterful wines. In this the Caseys have not been disappointed. Flavor and nose are both marked in these wines.

A volume of 1000 cases each of Chardonnay and Cabernet Sauvignon is the planned output, with no idea of ever outgrowing the present quarters.

Although there are no formal guest facilities, the Caseys will arrange for visits from dedicated wine anthusiasts by advance appointment.

Charles Krug Winery

This winery, said to be the oldest in Napa Valley, was established by Charles Krug in 1861. He was a pioneer wine man whose influence reached far beyond the valley. He was the first Viticultural Commissioner for the district of Napa, and was known for his prodigality of sympathy, kindliness and geniality. In his day the winery was known as "Chateau Krug," with its majestic oaks, old-time rambling buildings and air of homely comfort.

Charles Krug was born in Prussia, emigrated to the USA at age 22, and then returned to his native land briefly to participate in an atempt to overthrow a reactionary government. The revolt failed, Krug was imprisoned, but made a dramatic escape and fled to Philadelphia, pursued by state police.

Krug came to San Francisco in 1852 and worked on a newspaper there until he met Agoston Haraszthy, who influenced him to get into viticulture. He bought 20 acres in Sonoma County and planted vines. That same year, using a small cider press, he made 1200 gallons of wine in Napa Valley. This established him as a proficient winemaker, and his services were in demand.

In 1860 he moved to St. Helena and settled on the present winery site, where he planted a vineyard and built his first wine callar. One stone wall of this original winery is still standing.

Krug was a California wine enthusiast, devoted whole-heartedly to upgrading the industry. Never daunted by phylloxera, depression or past blunders, he gave his life and an ample fortune to developing the industry and improving the wines. Fortunately he lived to see Napa Valley lead the state in production of fine wines. With his dedication to all that was progressive, he left a legacy of high standards in conduct and achievements to the industry.

After his death the ranch was run by his two daughters, Lolita and Linda, and later by a nephew, who made wine up to the time of Prohibition. After Repeal, the vineyards and cellars were leased to Napa Wine Co. until they were sold to the Cesare Mondavi family in 1943.

The operation has been in the hands of the Mondavis ever since that time. Cesare was an Italian immigrant who came to America and worked in the iron mines in Minnesota. He returned to Italy to marry his childhood sweetheart and bring her back to the U.S.A. Their four children, Mary, Helen, Robert and Peter, were born in the mid-west.

In 1922 Cesare came to California, settling at Lodi and going into the wholesale fruit business, a successful venture. When Repeal came he was ready to begin winemaking, and looked about for a location in Napa Valley, where he shrewdly deemed the future of fine wines lay. Both his sons had studied enology, and he was thinking of their future. The Sunny St. Helena Winery, at the south edge of town, was first acquired and added to his operations at Lodi and Fresno. Later he purchased the Krug estate, and the family faced together the challenge of rehabilitation and expanding the winery. It was at

6000 oak barrels stacked for aging.

this juncture that the Mondavis realized their ambition of converting their operation from a bulk winery to one of bottled premium varietal wines. Old vineyards were pulled out, and vines replaced with better quality varieties. His wines began to receive recognition.

At his death in 1959, his heirs owned one of the finest and best equipped wineries in the country. Rosa Mondavi took her husband's place as head of the family and president of C. Mondavi & Sons until her death in 1976. Peter, a graduate of Stanford University with degrees in viticulture and enology, succeeded her as president and general manager, with the other Mondavi childrn as owners and directors of the family corporation. Peter is also the winemaker, assisted by George Vierra.

In the 34-odd years of Mondavi ownership there as the best way to achieve fine wines of consistent high quality. The winery, although large (3,500,000 storage capacity) has kept the individual touch, and a glow of pride in achievement that is immediately felt at the winery.

In the 30-odd years of Mondavi ownership there have been some changes. The size, scope and efficiency of the cellars have been greatly augmented, with the most up-to-date equipment and modern technology introduced. Additional acreage has been acquired and planted to the finest varietals, with 1500 acres in Napa Valley planted to Cabernet Sauvignon, Pinot Noir, Gamay Beaujolais, Pinot Chardonnay, Johannisberg Riesling and Gewurztraminer.

In 1966, Robert Mondavi left the firm to establish his own winery further down the valley. Peter remains to hold Mondavi aims, policies and goals to the high standard set by his father, and before him, by Charles Krug.

"To make fine wine, there must be modern equipment and technology," says Peter Mondavi, "and also the human element must be maintained. The old-timers believed and quality of the man's wine depended on his own quality and character. A little bit of himself goes into every bottle. To gain lasting fame, a winemaker must be a poet, a philosopher, an honorable man, as well as a master craftsman."

Two labels are used at Charles Krug Winery, the Charles Krug brand of varietal and generic wines bottled in fifths and tenths, and the CK brand, varietal and generic wines available in these sizes and also in gallons and half-gallons. Wines are distributed nationally.

The advance of dry winemaking technology in this area, says Peter, has attracted and continues to attract the best winemakers. If those establishing wineries in the valley do the right job, planting the right grapes in the right area, with a winemaker who can put it all together, their wines will always find a market. However, he points out, people entering the industry should realize that establishing a label takes many years, years filled with hard work and frustration.

It is rumored that the family has turned down some tempting offers to sell out. They continue to resist, for the feeling for the traditions of an old family winery is strong in the Mondavi clan.

The winery buildings are of turn-of-the century vintage, and music festivals and many other community events are held each year on its wide, oak-fringed lawns.

Conn Creek Winery

This new winery at 3222 Ehlers Lane, St. Helena, occupies quarters in an old stone winery that is a valley landmark. It bears on its facade the name of its builder and the year, "B. Ehler, 1886".

Owners of the winery are William and Kathleen Collins and William and May Beaver. They lease the handsome old stone building from its present owner, Michael Casey. It had stood idle since 1958. From 1932, at Repeal, until 1958, it had been operated by a former owner, Fred Domingos, as the Old Mill Winery. Generic wines were made and sold at the winery to patrons bringing their own jugs to be filled. This was a common practice among valley wineries attempting to get on their feet in the difficult years after the repeal of Prohibition.

The present owners put down a new concrete floor in the building, and installed equipment purchased from the now defunct Lyncrest Winery. They also purchased the Lyncrest wine inventory. Refrigeration and air conditioning have been added.

Bill Collins has been a grower in Napa Valley for the past 10 years. His vineyards, including two through which Conn Creek flows, are planted to Zinfandel, Cabernet Sauvignon, Carignane, Barbera, Sauvignon Vert, Chardonnay and Gamay Beaujolais. From these vines, approximately 12,000 to 14,000 cases annually will be produced.

The building itself is of warm, locally cut stone, pinkish-tan in color at the front and side-fronts, shading to darker stone at rear and rear sides of the structure. Arched windows add to its other-century appearance. Conn Creek Vineyards occupies the building on a long-term lease, and will some day build its own winery, says Collins. In the meantime, the present quarters suffice very well for all the winery work and storage.

Winemaker is John Henderson, another legacy from Lyncrest. He was formerly winemaker at Souverain Cellars under the prestigious Leland Stewart regime. Wine Consultant Brad Webb, who is identified with such gilt-edged wineries as Hanzell in Sonoma County and Freemark Abbey in Napa County, is their consultant as they get the new Conn Creek wines under way.

The first crush was made in 1976, and consisted of Zinfandel, Cabernet Sauvignon and White Riesling. Chardonnay and Gamay Beaujolais will also be made commencing in 1977.

Collins, who operates the vineyard while retaining his post as President of an electronics company, and Bill Beaver, an Adjunct Professor at Stanford, intend to age their Cabernet and Zinfandel for a minimum of two and probably three years.

The winery is situated on a tree-shaded knoll, easily visible from Highway 29. Around the premises are old pieces of winery equipment which Collins plans to restore as items of interest to present day visitors. An even earlier piece of equipment, dating back to pre-vineyard days when wheat was one of the valley's important crops, is a steam-powered threshing machine. This will also be restored as a relic of an older day.

Burgess Cellars

A hand-carved wooden sign on the western slopes of Howell Mountain, northeast of St. Helena, marks the entrance to Burgess Cellars. It occupies a stone and redwood winery building constructed in 1875. The winery site is at about 1000 feet elevation, and is a part of the original Rossini homestead.

The property was purchased in 1943 by J. Leland Stewart, a former advertising man, who founded the original Souverain Cellars. Stewart restored the 30-acre vineyad, remodeled and enlarged the winery, and commissioned the handsome carved wooden doors, the work of artist Merrill Abbot. More buildings were added for storing and aging the wines. Stewart learned the art of winemaking with the help of University of California enologists and his Napa Valley vintner neighbors, among them Grand Vintner Andre Tchelistcheff. During the next few years, the cellars became identified with a reputation for excellence in their wines.

Aftr 25 successful vintages, Stewart sold the winery in 1970, and in 1972 it became the property of Tom and Linda Burgess, former New Yorkers. The Burgesses were avid wine buffs in Hopewell Junction, New York state. Tom, a former corporation airplane pilot, and Linda, who had traveled extensively, found the small winery on Howell Mountain the ideal spot for them to pursue a life style attractive to both, plus a fascinating and rewarding career.

Winemaking at Burgess Cellars has been in the capable hands of Bill Sorenson, a native of Missouri. His background includes having charge of the experimental winery at California State University, Fresno, during his undergraduate years. He says: "Each of the vintages since 1972 has been unique. Each wine is made to enhance its special characteristics."

Burgess Cellars wines are made from plantings on their own acres, plus grapes bought from selected vineyards in the area. Tom has sought out growers who are as anxious to have their grapes achieve their full potential as Burgess Cellars is to guide them to greatness. In the making of fine wines, the Burgess philosophy is: "To make great wines, you need great grapes."

Sorenson believes that fermenting white wines in oak casks adds character unobtainable by any other method. Red wines are aged in American oak until they have completed malolactic fermentation. This, he believes, gives the winemaker maximum control over these delicate phases of winemaking.

Production remains small, about 15,000 cases annually of premium Cabernet Sauvignon, Johannisberg Riesling, Zinfandel, Chardonnay, Petite Sirah, Chenin Blanc Dry and Green Hungarian. These wines are limited in quantity, because this dedicated family operation is concerned with producing only fine varietal wines. This is the Burgess goal, coupled with the desire to continue life of a family deeply involved with wine.

Most of the time the winery is open for informal touring. Patrons are invited to picnic above the winery and enjoy a panoramic view of the entire northern Napa Valley and surrounding mountains.

Pope Valley Winery

POPE VALLEY
ZINFANDEL
ROSÉ NOUVEAU
1974 NAPA VALLEY

A young, fruity and very dry wine. From
Pope Valley vineyards. Limited release
in February, 1975, of only 648 bottles.

Produced and bottled by Pope Valley Winery, Napa County, Ca 94567
ALCOHOL 12% BY VOLUME

This rustic building on Pope Valley Road is one of the few gravity flow wineries left in California. It is three stories high, built into the hillside behind, taking advantage of the terrain for temperature control.

The winery was founded by Sam Haus in 1909, and operated with his sister Lily under the name "Sam Haus Winery" until his retirement in 1959. Sam achieved a certain local distinction for his undying war on rattlesnakes; now retired, he still pursues them relentlessly on trips to the country.

After his retirement, the winery was idle until 1972, when it was bought by its present owners, James and Arlene Devitt.

The winery represents a bit of old California history. Its timbers are of redwood, salvaged from the old Oat Hill Mine, a Napa County quicksilver mine of the 1880's. This mine was located near the Mountain Mill House, now a Girl Scout camp, which was then a stagecoach relay stop and inn for travelers to Lake County. The setting is picturesque, among valley oaks, built partly over a live stream. The Devitts have completely renovated the building, replacing all equipment and cooperage with new, modern fittings, yet still retaining the natural charm.

In its early days the building was designed to receive grapes on the top (third) floor. They were then conveyed to the second floor, where the crusher and fermenters were located. After its fermentation period, the wine was racked, by gravity, into storage tanks in the cellar on the first floor. Here the wine was aged before being racked once more into smaller 50-gallon barrels for shipment to eastern markets for bottling and distribution.

Today the procedure is the same, except that wines are aged in small cooperage, and bottled at the winery. Some wines have been released in Northern and Southern California as well as at the winery and the Pope Valley General Store. Capacity of the winery is 60,000 gallons storage. Wines include generic and varietal types.

The winery has another claim to fame, which makes it relatively easy to locate—it is across the road from another valley landmark, the Litto Damonte place. This folk artist has fashioned a setting from thousands of old hub caps, spiced with old tires, washing machines, plumbing fixtures, bird houses, windmills and wishing wells. Once seen it can never be forgotton, and the creator of this masterpiece enjoys having visitors stop in to chat and exclaim.

Devitt, a former hobby winemaker, is still involved with his electronics business, but expects to become a full time winemaker in due course. The winery is open on weekends, and is a pleasant place to visit, with picnic tables, hiking area and renovated blacksmith shop. The Devitts are proud to point out the ranch was entirely self sufficient in the past and the old steam boiler which once powered the ranch can still be seen. Interested wine buffs may drop in to talk with the proprietor, taste and buy available vintages. An aura of timelessness prevails, reminiscent of an earlier, simpler day.

Freemark Abbey Winery

Freemark Abbey Winery was built in 1895 by Antonio Forni, a newly-arrived Italian, who used blocks of stone cut by hand from the surrounding area. He called his winery "Lombarda Cellars", and continued operations until 1922, when it was sold to Patrick Murphy and James J. Mahoney. In 1938 it reverted to the widow of the founder, who sold it to Albert M. Ahern. Ahern first called the winery "Freemark Abbey".

In 1965 the property, then owned by Ben Swig of hotel fame and no longer operated as a winery, was sold to the present owners, a limited partnership involving seven men. They reactivated the winery in 1967. Charles Carpy, one of the owners, is a grandson of an earlier Charles Carpy, who operated the Uncle Sam Wine Cellars at Napa in the 1880's.

Other local owner-growers are Frank Wood, William Jaeger, James Warren, wine consultant Brad Webb, and Richard Heggie and John Bryan of the Bay Area. Winemaker is Larry Langen, a graduate of California State University at Davis.

The new owners planted choice varietals in two vineyards in the Rutherford area, Red Barn Ranch and the Carpy-Woods vineyards. From the start they were interested in producing fine wine by as natural methods as possible. Their operation is based on the concept "Control the environment, and let the wine make itself."

They prefer to minimize filterings, heavy fining and extreme stabilization procedures in an effort to retain all the flavor inherent in the grapes, and to accent vintage variations. Red wines are aged in small oak cooperage from 18 to 24 months, released four years after vintage. Whites are released two years after vintage, with nine months to a year of bottle age.

Wines are made to fit the grapes, and consequently vary from year to year in style. Although adhering closely to traditional methods of vinification, Freemark Abbey likes to be innovative too, attempting to achieve full potential from each vintage.

Production at Freemark Abbey amounts to some 20,000 cases annually, comprising five varieties: Cabernet Sauvignon, Chardonnay, Pinot Noir, Johannisberg Riesling and Petite Sirah. Limited distribution reaches thirty states.

The mossy stone cellar houses a restaurant, gourmet shop and candle factory on the upper floor, none of which are winery-related. The winery proper occupies the lower floor, and a handsome new facility at the side-rear is used for bottle storage, laboratory, visitor accommodations and retail sales room.

Although Freemark Abbey is a relatively new winery, the owners have made some wines which have been compared favorably with the finest French vintages. Harry Waugh, the British connoisseur, calls their 1968 Cabernet Bosche (from a special vineyard), "a splendid achievement". Their 1973 Edelwein, a naturally sweet Johannisberg Riesling, won outstanding national acclaim.

Stony Hill Vineyards

Fred and Eleanor McCrea established this small but exceedingly prestigious operation in 1951, and have since marketed wine to a small clientele reached via their own mailing list. Rare wineshops may occasionally have a few bottles, but they are few and far between. Each year's wines, two or three superb whites, are announced in early fall, released about November, and sold immediately. There is never enough to fill the great demand. These wines are said to be the best of their types grown in the area. Interested buyers are prompted to order them well in advance to insure delivery.

The winery and home are situated at the crest of an oak clad hill, seven hundred feet up in the Mayacamas Range, between Diamond Mountain on the north and Spring Mountain on the south, reached only by a winding road. The winemaker at Stony Hill is Michael Chelini. There are no tasting facilities open to the public, but those with a previous appointment may visit the winery.

Stony Hill and its production have remained small over the years by the owners' choice. This is one of the most inspiring operations in California winemaking history, and the vineyard and winery have prompted many others to try the same kind of preferred life style and business combined. The 30 acres of vines are planted on hillsides, with their roots in thin, rocky soil, and there is no irrigation or frost control. The vineyard is in a warm belt, protected by the contour of the land.

McCrea is one of the pioneer escapees from big business, coming to the valley in 1943 to establish a summer home. He was an advertising agency executive who knew nothing of winemaking. He determined to use the extra space to grow something, and on the advice of his neighbors, settled on grapes. He sought help from the University of California, who advised him to plant Chardonnay. His 30 acres are planted to Chardonnay, White Riesling, Traminer and Semillon.

The Napa Valley felt a sense of loss when on New Year's day, 1977, Fred McCrea quietly and unexpectedly died. He, along with the elder Louis Martini, had been the dean of family winemakers in this valley. His wife and family hope to carry on the tradition.

Over the years the McCreas planted, grew grapes, and made their first wines in the family kitchen, experimenting until the results satisfied them that they were ready to open the winery, a small building over the hill from the vineyards. Fred gives a high rating to established Napa Valley vintners who came to his assistance in those first years of winemaking, which resulted in some outstanding vintages laid down over the years. The advice to plant Chardonnay proved sound, and he had the satisfaction of seeing his two-year-old Chardonnay receive a Gold Medal at the California State Fair.

Aging of the Stony Hill white wines is done in small French and German oak cooperage, with a total capacity of about 7,000 gallons.

Stony Hill is a tiny winery, one of the smallest in Napa Valley, but it has had a great influence on the industry here and has acquired a well-deserved fame.

Kornell Champagne Cellars

This winery, built in the 1880's by the Salmina family who operated it as the Larkmead Winery for many distinguished years, has had several owners since, and it later became Larkmead Cooperative Winery.

Hanns Kornell, fourth generation of a champagne-making family, brought his champagne operation to the valley after eight years in Sonoma County. He married a Napa Valley girl, Marilouise Rossini, and the couple, with their young son and daughter, form another of the valley's totally involved winery families. Paula serves as a wine tour guide, and young Peter Hanns, not yet in his teens, opens wine, sits in on tastings and selections, and hands visitors his own business card with aplomb.

Hanns came from Germany, where he worked in the champagne vineyards and cellars of both his father and grandfather. He left in 1939, arriving in this country, as he likes to say, "with $2 and an old suitcase." He studied at Geisenheim Enological Institute, and later worked at winemaking in France, Italy and England. He hitchhiked from New York to California, where he worked first as a laborer, later at Fountaingrove winery in Sonoma County. From this humble start he has made himself one of the state's most respected champagne makers, with more than one and one half million bottles in various stages of development. In 1952 he leased an old winery, made champagne by night and sold it by day, until he had enough money to buy Larkmead, now Kornell Cellars.

The winery is a square cement building, with the same forthright stability as its owner. Hanns believes in good grapes as the foundation of all he is trying to do, and chooses with religious devotion the still wines from which he makes his cuvees—Riesling, Chardonnay, White Pinot and Semillon. He has no vineyards, buys grapes and wines, and from them makes champagne in the traditional "in this bottle" method. His Sehr Trocken is the most dry, made by extra long aging from a specially developed cuvee, and has won plaudits since its appearance in 1972. Blending, a good palate, and training from early youth by grandfather, father and uncles is the secret of the Kornell champagne success.

There is also Kornell himself, who brings to champagne making all the vigor and elan of the bubbly itself. He enjoys what he is doing, asks no more of life than that it permit him to go on making and enjoying champagnes with his family. He has a tremendous faith in the future of the valley as a great and enduring wine country. He finds no generation gap with youth, his own or those hired for the winery; he is a brisk, efficient employer who expects, and gets, the best from his employees.

He is a winemaker in the old tradition, the tradition of Jacob Schram and Gustave Niebaum. He prefers to work for himself, with all this implies for a small business today, and to be independent, his own man in his own setting. He has cheerfully refused many offers, some of fantastic proportions, to sell his winery, and hopes to have his children continue after him.

Schramsberg Vineyards

Jacob Schram came to America in 1842, and reached Napa Valley in 1862. He worked as an itinerant barber, but had his mind on wine. Soon the barber had saved enough money to acquire a mountainside of his own. His wife Annie and the hard working Chinese planted the vines while Jacob went from farm to farm, plying his scissors.

Hard work paid off. He built the sturdy Victorian house, capacious stables, and extensive caves. Robert Louis Stevenson visited him in 1880 and said he looked "the picture of prosperity." The engaging tale is told in "The Silverado Squatters." His wines gained acclaim, and were served at famous hotels and clubs in California and abroad.

Schram died in March 1905 and was succeeded by his son Herman, who operated the winery until Prohibition, when it was sold for a summer home. After Repeal and two abortive ownerships, it was purchased by the Jack Davies organization in 1965.

A young career man on his way up, Jack Davies met the San Francisco Wine and Food Society and his gourmet wife Jamie in the 1950's. These events marked the beginning of his lifelong affinity for elegant wines.

Friends took the couple to visit Martin Ray in Saratoga, an unforgettable experience. Their host appeared to welcome them, "looking like Bacchus and acting like Bacchus," Davies recalls. They sat down to luncheon, which merged into dinner with no visible line of demarcation. Champagne flowed freely. "The occasion burned itself into my memory," says Davies, who later became an investor in Ray's Mt. Eden Vineyards.

Seeking a similar way of life for himself, he decided to leave Los Angeles and the big business scene for a vineyard of his own. A visit to Napa Valley and to Schramsberg ended his search for the right place. It was plentifully supplied with caves; champagne seemed the answer. Help came from such knowledgeable wine men as Fred McCrea, Andre and Dmitri Tchelistcheff and Dr. Maynard Amerine. He was impressed with the Stony Hill operation; the quality of the wines, the uncompromising excellence this small enterprise had achieved. He saw a great opportunity to make an American champagne with the prestige of the French.

By shrewd management and hard work, Davies has made champagne that occupies a place of honor in the world of fine wine. He and Jamie have restored the fine old house; he has been busy with endless details of vinyard and cellars, purchasing, shipping, planning. He finds the life as satisfying as he had envisioned it to be. Wine, he believes, brings back to life something that has been slipping away, and he is determined not to lose that something, for himself and for his family.

To succeed as a small winery, he says, one must know what he wants to do and how he is going to do it, and not try to have a foot in both camps. His goal: As wide distribution as possible of a smallish amount of superlative champagne. "If we get big enough to cut per-unit cost appreciably," he says, "we will have lost our reason for being—uniqueness."

Stonegate Winery

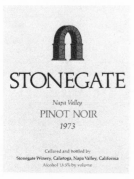

STONEGATE

Napa Valley
PINOT NOIR
1973

Cellared and bottled by
Stonegate Winery, Calistoga, Napa Valley, California
Alcohol 13.5% by volume

Stonegate, one of the new generation of small premium wineries in Napa Valley, is just off Highway 29 south of Calistoga on Dunaweal Lane, the road that leads to its much larger hilltop neighbor, Sterling. Stonegate was founded in 1973 by James and Barbara Spaulding of Berkeley, whose intent was to make premium varietal wines from their own vineyards.

The original Spaulding vineyard, planted several years before they started the winery, lies on steep hillsides west of Calistoga, at altitudes from 800 to 1000 feet. It consists of 15 acres of Cabernet Sauvignon, Merlot and Chardonnay. The vineyard on the winery property in the valley is planted to Pinot Noir, Sauvignon Blanc and Chardonnay. In addition, Stonegate makes Chenin Blanc, Zinfandel and Petite Sirah from a nearby vineyard on Silverado Trail.

The 17-acre winery property has, besides the winery, a farmhouse, barn and garage. The winery occupies a fame structure 24 by 72 feet, orginally built to house farm equipment. Now insulated and remodeled, it contains the winery office, laboratory, barrel aging room and cellar. Adjoining it is a concrete pad with nine of the winery's 13 stainless steel fermentation tanks (four are in the cellar), and the hopper, stemmer-crusher, press and chiller. Equipment has been carefully chosen to utilize the latest knowledge on fermentation and aging. The Spauldings respect the centuries-old tradition of European winemaking, handling the grapes with care,

and using a minimum of processing.

Stonegate wine is aged in European oak tanks and American and French oak barrels, about 25 percent of which are stacked in racks in a section of the 100-year-old farmhouse. The remainder of the house is occupied by the Spaulding's son, David, manager of Stonegate.

Jim Spaulding teaches journalism at the University of California, Berkeley. The family came to California in 1969 from Wisconsin, where Spaulding had been a medical science writer for the Milwaukee Journal. As a boy he worked in his father's vineyard in southwestern Michigan, and in Wisconsin his interest in wine led to experiments in growing French hybrids from New York State and European varieties from UC Davis.

The other full-time staff member is Fred Payne, a chemist with experience in other small premium wineries in Napa Valley. David, Fred, Barbara and Jim do most of the work of the winery and vineyards. Part time help is needed for pruning, and for bottling and labeling, which are hand operations.

Most of the wines of Stonegate are estate bottled, some from hillside vineyards, some from the valley floor. The winery is engineered to crush up to 500 tons annually, but the owners plan to stay near the 85-ton level (about 5,000 cases) for the present.

Stonegate is a small premium winery, carefully geared to improve and upgrade wine quality and to promote ease of operation. Its small size precludes wine tasting, but tours of the premises may be arranged by appointment, and the available wines are on sale at the winery.

Sterling Vineyards

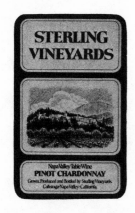

Sterling Vineyards, near Calistoga, was founded in 1964 by Sterling International, a paper company with factories in many part of the world. It is owned by four families, Peter L. Newton, Michael P. W. Stone, Michael Stock and Frank Tatum.

The project had its beginnings when the men of Sterling decided they wanted to own some land. They looked about, discovered Napa Valley, and established summer homes.

After some exposure to the wine industry, they were intrigued by it. They visited the University at Davis, viewed operations in South Africa and Australia. They decided that, by applying sound business principles, they could succeed in the wine industry. Land was acquired and planted to fine varietal grapes; vineyards consist of 400 acres in the upper valley, within three miles of the winery.

By 1968 they had enough vineyards to insure a supply of quality grapes, and began to study ideas for the winery. They had in mind something suited to the site, with esthetic appeal, not a hobby winery but a profitable business operation. A 100,000 case winery seemed about right.

The building that evolved is unique. The site is one of great natural beauty, a wood-fringed knoll between Silverado Trail and Highway 29. The building is the concept of Martin Waterfield, who wanted to recall the architecture of the Mediterranean. It is a simple, white structure, entirely functional, taking advantage of site possibilities to give California's most picturesque wine valley a creation of dignity and charm. There is a hint of the monastic, with stained glass windows, arches, carved doors and bells. The first plan was to top the building with a dove-cote, but this idea was discarded for bell towers in the interests of sanitation. The bells were cast in 1740, and once pealed from St. Dunstan's-in-the-East, London. The winery is reached by tram-cars from the valley. The yellow gondolas, transporting four visitors at a time, are now a familiar valley sight.

Sterling is one of the few Napa Valley wineries to be completely visitor-oriented from its inception. The interior is functional, with hospitality in mind. Visitors making the no-guide tour may view operations in the winery from a walkway above. A large upper deck commands a sweeping view of vine-clad valley and hills, and community functions are held there. There is something to delight all of the senses—the trees, fountains, bells, sculpture and flowers, plus the pungent smell of wine sleeping in tanks and barrels. The tasting room, farthest up the slope, has a roofed deck for enjoying the dramatic view.

The array of winemaking equipment is impressive. The latest and best of equipment and technology are employed by enologist R. W. Forman who, produced his first vintage in 1969, one year after receiving his masters degree at U.C. Davis. From its inception, the winery promised to produce some outstanding and innovative wines, and Forman, has justified the hopes placed in him by the Sterling owners.

Cuvaison Cellars

This is a new winery on Silverado Trail near Calistoga, topping a little rise on the east side of the valley. The Mission style building with its red tile roof is picturesque against the green hillside, and its stained glass windows, of modern design, duplicate the winery label. Terracing and landscaping are still going on at the site, and at the smaller hospitality center at the front of the property.

Cuvaison, which is a French word meaning the fermenting of red wines on the skins of grapes, was founded in 1970 by Thomas Cottrell and Thomas Parkhill, two young engineers from the San Jose area who had learned to love wine and wanted to become involved with it on a more intimate basis. They purchased the property, together with a 27-acre vineyard at Calistoga, and made their first crush the same year—1970.

Neither of these men are presently associated with Cuvaison, which is now the property of a new owner, Oakleigh Thorne, of New York. Under the new regime, changes are being made as rapidly as possible to carry out the winemaking theories and policies of the new winemaker, Philip Togni, formerly associated for eight years with Chappellet Vineyards.

Togni is known for his proficiency in his craft. He began his professional career in France, where he was identified with Chateau Lascombes, Bordeaux. He later worked in vineyards and wineries in Algeria and in Chile. He was with E. & J. Gallo on first coming to the USA, later moving to Napa Valley, where he worked with Donn Chappellet in the building and establishment of his winery and vineyards.

Togni believes that a winemaker must "have one foot in the vineyard, the other in the winery." At Cuvaison, where he served as consultant before becoming full-time winemaker, he has been given a free hand in planning for future great vintages. This has resulted in numerous changes in the physical plant. There is new French oak cooperage—they plan to use new wood every year for aging the wines—new bottling equipment, new crushing and fermenting facilities, all of the latest design and highest quality. A new concrete pad has been poured over the old one, new equipment placed on it, and a temperature controlled building, the same architectural style as the winery, is being constructed over the entire fermenting area.

As Winston Wilson, Cuvaison's public relations head, remarks, "Everything is from scratch, everything the best in Togni's opinion, and the owner has complete reliance on his judgment. We will limit our production to the three wines Philip believes are his best— Chardonnay, Cabernet Sauvignon and Zinfandel." The vineyard will be sold, and carefully selected grapes purchased by Togni from some of the valley vineyards.

The hospitality center, open Thursdays through Mondays, invites tasting of wines by patrons. The building is surrounded by wide decking that sprouts bright umbrellas in summer for outdoor wine tasting and picnicking.

171

Diamond Creek Vineyards

Albert Brounstein, a former owner of Standard Drug Distributors in Los Angeles and marketing man for Sebastiani and Weibel, bought and cleared the land on Diamond Creek six years ago. He has planted the 20 acres entirely to Cabernet Sauvignon and a small amount of Merlot for blending.

Al found, by soil analysis, three distinct soil types on the property, and the grapes from each will be made into three different estate-bottled Cabernet Sauvignons. The three are called Red Rock Terrace, Volcanic Hill and Gravelly Meadow vineyards, respectively, and each "vineyard within a vineyard" will have its own special label, showing the soil of origin.

Fermenting is done in redwood, aging in Nevers oak, and the wines are neither fined nor filtered.

By 1976 there will be some 3000 gallons ready to release. The first vintage, 1972, was released in 1974, and is already committed to purchasers, except for a small amount retained for the Brounsteins and their friends.

Al and Boots Brounstein believe in the valley with fervor, especially their own corner of it, as the place to produce Cabernet Sauvignon, that most exquisite product of the noble vines. Youth, dedication and zeal are involved in their venture.

Their theories of marketing are their own, and include inviting groups of wine-oriented people to picnic on a woodland lake, created by damming Diamond Creek. The lake, with its grassy tree-shaded banks, is picturesque and invites swimming and boating as an adjunct to partaking of good food and wine. After exposure to the charms of the zestful Brounsteins and their outdoor guest facilities, visitors may place their names on a mailing list, to be informed when wines are ready to be released. Al estimates the increase in customers needed each year to sell all the wine produced numbers in the hundreds and based entirely upon Diamond Creek's bearing acreage. The output will never be large, and will be limited exclusively to their Cabernet Sauvignon.

At present the Brounsteins are renting an old stone winery from a neighboring rancher. The building was constructed by Chinese laborers, and its facade bears the date "1888." After years of disuse, the Brounsteins cleared the building for their own wines, and are now aging two vintages in its root-tangled stone caves cut 100 feet back into the hills. It is naturally cool, the two-foot thick stone walls never allowing the temperature to rise above 60 degrees, nor fall below 55.

However, they are eager to get to work on their own winery, and are scheduled to begin its construction in 1976.

The new winery building, of stone and redwood, will, when complete, be tucked into a niche between two earthen hillocks and will provide them with quarters on its upper floor. Al likes to think of it as being designed along the same functional lines as Hanzell Winery. The site overlooks the vineyards, and is ringed about by woods of pine, fir, madrone and considerable stand of fine second-growth redwoods.

Chateau Montelena

Chateau Montelena, at the foot of Mount St. Helena in Calistoga, has a spectacular setting. It is an old winery, the label dating back to 1882. It was constructed by Alfred A. Tubbs, a New Englander who came from New York to California in 1850, and founded the Tubbs Cordage Company of San Francisco. He later became a California state senator. In 1880 he purchased 275 acres of Napa Valley land, planted a vineyard, and two years later built the winery.

A handsome mansion, Hillcrest, was built on top of a wooded hill—this was the Tubbs family country seat. (This beautiful landmark was burned to the ground in 1964.) Tubbs traveled to France, where he purchased cuttings from the most famous vineyards. He found much to admire in the architecture of their wineries, and when he returned home, using French stone masons and plans drawn by a French architect, the winery was constructed. Its facade is of imported cut stone; the rear and sides of native stone. It is, in the manner of that day, without steel reinforcing, its walls 42 inches thick at the rear, where it extends into the hillside—"built like a dam," says Lee Paschich, its present owner.

In 1886, Tubbs secured the services of French-born and trained Jerome Bardot as cellarmaster. He was a dedicated winemaker, and produced some outstanding vintages.

After the death of Alfred Tubbs in 1897, the winery was operated by his son William until 1919, when a grandson, Chapin F. Tubbs, took over the family holdings. Prohibition was the order of the day; vineyards were pulled out and orchards of pear and prune trees were planted. The winery fell into disuse for more than three decades.

In 1958, the estate was purchased by a Chinese couple, the Yort Franks. The Franks created a five-acre lake, with three islands crowned with red lacquer pavilions, curving bridges and an authentic Chinese junk. Weeping willows fringed the beautiful water gardens, and Frank re-named the estate, poetically, Jade Gardens. It was their family home until 1968, when it was sold to Lee Paschich.

In 1972 the new owner acquired two partners, James L. Barrett and Ernest W. Hahn, and reopened the winery. Chateau Montelena was furnished and equipped with modern winemaking equipment, and the services of a dedicated winemaker were enlisted—Miljenko (Mike) Grgich. Grgich is a Croatian-born enologist who received his training at the University of Zagreb in Jugoslavia. He came to the USA in 1958, worked for a time under American enologists at some of Napa Valley's most prestigious wineries.

Grgich is a conscientious winemaker with an enviable background, and believes firmly in the future of the valley and its wines. California winemaking has come of age, he says. "A new level of quality has been reached—there are more good grapes, better cooperage, more know-how. There are more experienced growers and winemakers, more appreciative wine drinkers, and of course more money."

The Aging Caves at Schramsberg Cellars.

Other Wineries

NAPA VALLEY COOPERATIVE WINERY is a large, sprawling building south of the city of St. Helena. Their operation is exclusively that of making wine out of Napa Valley grapes for E. & J. Gallo, and sending it in tank trucks to Modesto. They have a large grower membership among valley viticulturists, and each grower is permitted to bottle enough of the resulting wine for his own use.

RUTHERFORD VINTNERS is a new wine-making endeavor located directly across Hwy. 29 from Franciscan Winery. Longtime Louis P. Martini Winery employee, Bernard Skoda, will release his first wine, a 1974 Cabernet Sauvignon, in 1977. Other wines produced are Johannisberg Riesling, Pinot Noir and Chardonnay.

SILVER OAKS CELLARS, a small bonded winery, has its aging cellars at 915 Oakville Crossroad, and is said by its owners, Justin Meyer and Raymond Duncan, to be the first winery in California producing Cabernet Sauvignon wine exclusively. The cellar was founded in 1972, and crushed its first vintage that year. Crushing and fermenting are done at Franciscan Winery, Highway 29 at Galleron Road, also owned by Meyer and Duncan. The 1972 Cabernet Sauvignon is now available at Franciscan. Capacity is 4000 cases.

STEWART SMITH and his brother Charles cleared their Spring Mountain peak property in 1971. They began replanting the old 1890's vineyards with Pinot Noir, Cabernet, Riesling and Chardonnay foreseeing an ultimate capacity of 6,000 cases annually. The estate bottled wines will be produced in their unique sod-roofed winery now under construction with the first crush in 1976.

SPOTTSWOODE CELLARS is owned by Jack R. Novak. This historic wine estate was originally built in 1883 and was called Lindenhurst. It was renamed by the second owner, Mrs. Spotts. Spottswoode was the property of the Belani family until 1968 and produced wines under the Montebello label until Novak acquired the winery in 1971. Total annual production will be limited to 15,000 cases with wines first released in 1976.

TULOCAY WINERY is located on Coombsville Road east of Napa. Owner Bill Cadman projects an eventual production of one thousand cases for this tiny premium wine operation. The first crush was in 1975, with the release of wines in 1978. The Cadmans have no vineyards of their own but selectively purchase grapes to produce Pinot Noir, Cabernet Sauvignon, Zinfandel and Chardonnay.

THE OWNERS OF VEEDERCREST WINERY are re-establishing vineyards on a 300-acre ranch in the Mayacamas mountains, at the intersection of Mt. Veeder and Lokoya Roads. Currently, the corporation operates a 900 case winery in the Bay Area, which they plan to move to Napa Valley within the next three years. The winery will then be expanded to a planned capacity of 20,000 cases annually. Alfred W. Baxter, president of the firm, serves as winemaker; Patrick Baker is ranch manager. Winery tours are available by appointment only.

Appendix

BEAULIEU VINEYARDS—Page 103
Address: 1960 Highway 29, Rutherford
Phone: (707) 963-3671
Hours: 10 to 4 daily
Facilities: Tours, tasting, retail sales
Winemaker: Theo Rosenbrand
Wines: generic, varietal, dessert and sparkling wines
Vineyards: 745 acres
Volume: 1,800,000 gallons storage

BERINGER WINERY—Page 139
Address: 2000 Main Street, St. Helena
Phone: (707) 963-7115
Hours: 9 to 4:45 daily
Facilities: tasting, tours, sales, gift shop
Winemaker: Myron Nightingale
Wines: varietal, generic, dessert, sparkling wines; brandy
Vineyards: 3,000 acres
Volume: 2.5 million gallons storage; 600,000 gallons
fermenting: 200,000 cases per year

BURGESS CELLARS—Page 155
Address: 1108 Deer Park Road, St. Helena
Phone: (707) 963-4766
Hours: 10-4 daily
Facilities: Sales, picnic area; informal tours; no tasting
Winemaker: Bill Sorenson
Wines: varietal and generic
Vineyards: 22 acres plus select purchased grapes
Volume: 15,000 cases per year, storage 80,000 gallons,
fermenting 9,000 gallons

CAKEBREAD CELLARS—Page 97
Address: 8300 St. Helena Highway, Rutherford
Phone: 963-9182, (415) 835-8463
Hours: not open to public except by appointment
Facilities: tours by appointment only
Winemaker: Jack Cakebread
Wines: Cabernet Sauvignon, Sauvignon Blanc, Chardonnay
Vineyards: 22 acres
Volume: 4,000 cases annually

CARNEROS CREEK WINERY—Page 73
Address: 1285 Dealy Lane, Napa
Phone: (707) 226-3279
Hours: open by appointment
Facilities: tours by appointment only
Winemaker: Francis Mahoney
Wines: Chardonnay, Cabernet, Pinot Noir, Zinfandel
Vineyards: 10 acres Pinot Noir plus select purchased grapes
Volume: 21,500 gallons fermenting, 10,000 cases annually

CAYMUS VINEYARDS—Page 107
Address: 8700 Conn Creek Road, St. Helena
Phone: (707) 963-4204
Hours: by appointment, case sales only
Facilities: Tasting
Winemaker: Charles Wagner
Wines: Pinot Noir, Pinot Noir Blanc, Cabernet, Johannis-
berg Riesling
Vineyards: 70 acres
Volume: 20,000 gallons

CHAPPELLET VINEYARDS—Page 111
Address: 1581 Sage Canyon Road, St. Helena
Phone: (707) 963-7136
Hours: by appointment only
Facilities: group tours by appointment, sales by mailing list
Winemaker: Joe Cafaro
Wines: Chenin Blanc, Johannisberg Riesling, Chardonnay,
Cabernet Sauvignon
Vineyards: 95 acres plus grapes from neighboring vineyards
Volume: 60,000 gallons storage

CHATEAU CHEVALIER—Page 133
Address: 3101 Spring Mountain Road, St. Helena
Phone: (707) 963-2342
Hours: by appointment only
Facilities: Advance appointment only
Winemaker: Gregory Bissonette
Wines: Cabernet, Chardonnay, Pinot Noir, White Riesling
Vineyards: 60 acres plus purchased grapes
Volume: 9,000 gallons fermenting, 4,000 cases annually

CHATEAU MONTELENA—Page 175
Address: 1429 Tubbs Lane, Calistoga
Phone: (707) 942-5105
Hours: 10-4, Mon.-Fri.
Facilities: group tours, appointment only, retail sales
Winemaker: Mike Grgich
Wines: Chardonnay, Johannisberg Riesling, Cabernet, Zinfandel
Vineyards: 100 acres plus purchased grapes
Volume: 75,000 gallons fermenting, 20,000 cases annually

CHRISTIAN BROTHERS WINERY—Page 143
Address: 2555 North Main Street, St. Helena
Phone: (707) 963-2719
Hours: 10 to 4 daily
Facilities: tours, tasting, retail sales
Winemaker: Brother Timothy
Wines: varietal, generic, dessert champagne, vermouth, brandy
Vineyards: 2,000 acres
Volume: 20,000,000 gals. storage, 3,100,00 fermentation

CLOS DU VAL—Page 81
Address: 5330 Silverado Trail, Napa
Phone: (707) 252-6711
Hours: production winery only
Facilities: By appointment only
Winemaker: Bernard Portet
Wines: Cabernet Sauvignon, Zinfandel
Vineyards: 120 acres
Volume: 12,000-14,000 cases annually; storage, fermenting

CONN CREEK WINERY—Page 153
Address: 3222 Ehlers Lane, St. Helena
Phone: 963-9100
Hours: not yet open to public
Facilities: tours by appointment
Winemaker: John Henderson
Wines: Zinfandel, Cabernet Sauvignon, White Riesling, other varietals
Volume: 12,000 to 14,000 cases annually

CUVAISON CELLARS—Page 171
Address: 4560 Silverado Trail North, Calistoga
Phone: (707) 942-6100
Hours: 10 to 4 daily
Facilities: tasting, picnic tables
Winemaker: Philip Togni
Wines: Chardonnay, Cabernet Sauvignon, Zinfandel
Vineyards: purchased grapes only
Volume: 20,000 cases annually

DIAMOND CREEK VINEYARDS—Page 173
Address: 1500 Diamond Mountain Road, Calistoga
Phone: (415) 346-3644
Hours: no visitor accommodations
Facilities: group tours and picnics by appointment only
Winemaker: Albert Brounstein
Wines: 3 distinct bottlings of Cabernet Sauvignon
Vineyards: 20 acres
Volume: 6,000 gallons fermenting, 1000 cases

DOMAINE CHANDON—Page 87
Address: California Drive, P.O. Box 2470, Yountville
Phone: (707) 944-8844
Hours: 11-6, closed Tuesday and Wednesday
Facilities: tours, tasting, retail sales, restaurant
   (banquets and private parties can be arranged)
Wines: sparkling wines
Vineyards: 900 acres
Volume: 100,000 cases

FRANCISCAN VINEYARDS—Page 115
Address: 1178 Galleron Road, St. Helena
Phone: (707) 963-7111
Hours: 10 to 4 daily
Facilities: self guided tour, sales
Winemaker: Justin Meyer
Wines: varietals
Vineyards: 1000 acres
Volume: 500,000 gallons, 70,000 cases annually

FREEMARK ABBEY WINERY—Page 159
Address: 3022 St. Helena Highway, St. Helena
Phone: (707) 963-7106
Hours: 11-4:30 for retail sales
Facilities: tours, M-F 11 & 2; weekends, 1:30 & 3
Winemaker: Larry Langen
Wines: varietal
Vineyards: 200 acres
Volume: 20,00 cases annually

HEITZ WINE CELLARS—Page 121
Address: 500 Taplin Road, St. Helena
Phone: (707) 963-3542
Hours: 11-4:30 at 436 Main Street, St. Helena
Facilities: tasting, retail sales at 436 Main St., St. Helena
Winemaker: Joseph Heitz
Wines: table, dessert and sparkling wines
Vineyards: 30 cares plus selected purchases
Volume: 85,000 gallons storage

INGLENOOK VINEYARDS—Page 99
Address: Highway 29, Rutherford
Phone: (707) 963-7182
Hours: 9-5 daily
Facilities: tasting, tours, sales gift shop
Winemaker: Thomas Farrell
Wines: generic, varietal, dessert and sparkling wines
Vineyards: 2800 acres
Volume: 3,000,000 plus gallons fermentation

HANNS KORNELL CHAMPAGNE CELLARS—Page 163
Address: 1091 Larkmead Lane, Calistoga
Phone: (707) 963-2334
Hours: 10 to 4:30 daily
Facilities: tasting, tours, sales gift shop
Winemaker: Hanns Kornell
Vineyards: none
Volume: 30,000 cases

CHARLES KRUG WINERY—Page 149
Address: Highway 29, St. Helena
Phone: (707) 963-2761
Hours: 10 to 4 daily
Facilities: tours, tasting, retail sales
Winemaker: Peter Mondavi
Wines: varietal, generic, Chas. Krug label; varietal, generic, CK label
Vineyards: 1500 acres
Volume: approx. 4 million gallons storage, 230,000 gallons fermentation

LOUIS MARTINI WINERY—Page 127
Address: 254 St. Helena Hwy., St. Helena
Phone: (707) 963-2736
Hours: 10 to 4 daily
Facilities: tours, tasting, retail sales
Winemaker: Louis P. Martini
Wines: varietal, generic, dessert wines
Vineyards: 800 acres
Volume: 500,000 gallons fermenting, 250,000 cases annually

MAYACAMAS VINEYARDS—Page 77
Address: 1155 Lokoya Road, Napa
Phone: (707) 224-4030
Hours: by appointment only
Facilities: retail sales, tours
Winemaker: Bob Travers
Wines: Cabernet Sauvignon, Chardonnay, Zinfandel
Vineyards: 45 acres plus purchased grapes
Volume: 5,000 cases annually, 12,000 gallons fermenting

ROBERT MONDAVI WINERY—Page 93
Address: 7801 Highway 29, Oakville
Phone: (707) 963-7156
Hours: 10:30 to 4 daily
Facilities: tours, tasting, retail sales
Winemaker: Robert Mondavi
Wines: varietals, generics
Vineyards: 750 acres plus purchased grapes
Volume: 1,200,000 gallons fermenting, 600,000 cases

MT. VEEDER WINERY—Page 75
Address: 1999 Mt. Veeder Road, Napa
Phone: (707) 224-4039
Hours: by appointment only
Facilities: tours, to be arranged
Winemaker: Kimbal Giles
Wines: Cabernet Sauvignon and Zinfandel
Vineyards: 20 acres
Volume: 7,000 gallons fermenting, 2,000 cases annually

NAPA WINE CELLARS—Page 89
Address: 7481 St. Helena Hwy., Oakville, Ca.
Phone: None yet
Hours: by appointment
Facilities: retail sales
Winemaker, Charles Woods
Wines: Cabernet, Chardonnay, Zinfandel
Vineyards: 3 acres plus selected purchased grapes
Volume: 5,000 gal. fermenting, 9500 gal. storage

NICHELINI VINEYARDS—Page 113
Address: Highway 128, St. Helena
Phone: (707) 963-3357
Hours: 10 to 6:00 p.m. weekends
Facilities: tasting, informal tours, sales, picnicking
Winemaker: James Nichelini
Wines: varietals
Vineyards: 200 acres
Volume: 50,000 gallons storage, 5,000 cases annually

JOSEPH PHELPS VINEYARDS—Page 119
Address: 200 Taplin Road, St. Helena
Phone: (707) 963-2745
Hours: M-S 8-5
Facilities: tours by appointment, retail sales
Winemaker: Walter Schug
Wines: varietals
Vineyards: 115 acres plus purchased local grapes
Volume: 240,000 gallons storage, 100,000 gallons fermenting

POPE VALLEY WINERY—Page 157
Address: 6613 Pope Valley Road, St. Helena
Phone: (707) 965-2192
Hours: 11-6 daily
Facilities: tasting, tours, sales, picnic tables, hiking
Winemaker: Robert & Steven Devitt
Wines: varietals and generics
Volume: 7,000 gallons fermenting, 4,000 cases annually

RAYMOND VINEYARDS AND CELLAR—Page 117
Address: 849 Zinfandel Lane, St. Helena
Phone: (707) 963-3141
Hours: not open to public
Facilities: tours of premises by appointment only
Winemaker: Roy Raymond
Wines: varietal
Vineyards: 90 acres
Vilume: 5,000 cases, volume 20,000 cases

RITCHIE CREEK VINEYARD—Page 137
Address: 4024 Spring Mtn. Road, St. Helena
Phone: (707) 963-4661
Hours: by appointment only
Facilities: none open to public
Winemaker: Peter Minor
Wines: Cabernet Sauvignon, Chardonnay
Vineyards: 4 acres
Volume: 700 cases annually

RUTHERFORD HILL—Page 109
Address: P.O. Box 410, Rutherford
Phone:
Hours: none at present
Facilities: none at present
Winemaker: Phil Baxter
Wines: varietal
Vineyards: not available
Volume: not available

ST. CLEMENT VINEYARDS—Page 147
Address: 2867 North St., St. Helena Hwy., St. Helena
Phone: 963-7221
Hours: not open to public except by appointment
Facilities: by appointment only
Winemaker: Robert Stemmler; assistant, Jon Axhelm
Wines: Cabernet Sauvignon, Chardonnay
Vineyards: 29 acres adjacent to home
Volume: 2,000 casses annually

V. SATTUI WINERY—Page 123
Address: White Lane, St. Helena, Ca.
Phone: (707) 963-7774
Hours: 10 to 4 daily, closed Mondays in winter
Facilities: tasting room, gift and gourmet shop, picnicking
Winemaker: Daryl Sattui
Wines: Cabernet Sauvignon and Zinfandel
Vineyards: grapes purchased
Volume: 5000 gallons

SCHRAMSBERG VINEYARD—Page 165
Address: Schramsberg Road, Calistoga
Phone: (707) 942-4558
Hours: by appointment only
Facilities: tours, retail sales
Winemaker: Harold Osborne
Wines: bottle fermented champagnes
Vineyards: 40 acres
Volume: 38,000 gallons fermentation, 500,000 bottles
aging, 14,000 cases annually

SILVER OAK CELLARS—Page 177
Address: 915 Oakville Crossroad, Oakville
Phone: 944-8866
Hours: not open to public
Facilities: tours by appointment only
Winemaker: Justin Meyer
Wines: Cabernet Sauvignon
Vineyards: no figure available
Volume: 4,000 cases annually

SPOTTSWOODE CELLARS—Page 177
Address: 1245 Hudson Ave., St. Helena
Phone: (707) 963-7433
Hours: by appointment
Facilities: by appointment
Winemaker: Jack Novak
Wines: Varietals
Vineyards: 75 acres
Volume: 12,000 gal. fermenting

SPRING MOUNTAIN VINEYARDS—Page 131
Address: 2805 Spring Mountain Road, St. Helena
Phone: (707) 963-4341
Hours: by appointment only
Facilities: none open to public
Winemaker: Charles Ortman
Wines: varietals only
Vineyards: 220 acres
Volume: 16,000 cases

STAG'S LEAP WINE CELLARS—Page 83
Address: 5766 Silverado Trail, Napa
Phone: (707) 255-4284
Hours: open by appointment only
Facilities: none, except as above
Winemaker: Warren Winiarski
Wines: varietals
Vineyards: 44 acres plus select purchased grapes
Volume: 50,000 gallons fermenting, 18,000 cases annually

STAG'S LEAP WINERY—Page 85
Address: Stag's Leap Ranch, Yountville
Phone: (707) 944-2792
Hours: not open to public
Facilities: sales by mailing list only
Winemaker: Carl Doumani
Wines: varietals
Vineyards: 100 acres
Volume: 50,000 gallons, 5,000 cases annually

STERLING VINEYARDS—Page 168
Address: 1111 Dunaweal Lane, Calistoga
Phone: (707) 942-5151
Hours: 10:30 to 5 daily, summer; 10:30 to 4:30 winter
Facilities: tasting, self-guided tours, sales
Winemaker: Ric Forman
Wines: varietals
Vineyards: 400 acres
Volume: 360,000 gallons storage, 109,000 gallons fermenting

STONEGATE WINERY—Page 167
Address: Dunaweal Lane, Calistoga
Phone: (707) 942-6500
Hours: 10 to 4 for sales
Tours: By appointment
Manager: David Spaulding
Wines: varietals
Vineyards: 30 acres
Volume: 48,000 gallons fermenting, 5,000 cases annually

STONY HILL VINEYARD—Page 161
Address: P.O. Box 308, St. Helena
Phone: (707) 963-2636
Hours: no regular hours
Facilities: visits arranged by written request
Winemaker: Michael Chelini
Wines: varietals
Vineyards: 30 acres
Volume: 8,700 gallons fermenting, 2,000 cases annually

SUTTER HOME WINERY—Page 125
Address: 277 St. Helena Highway, St. Helena
Phone: (707) 963-3104
Hours: 10 to 4:30
Facilities: tasting, retail sales
Winemaker: Bob Trinchero
Wines: varietal, generic, dessert; specialize in Zinfandel
Vineyards: none
Volume: 50,000 gallons fermenting, 20,000 cases

TREFETHEN VINEYARDS—Page 79
Address: 1060 Oak Knoll Rd., Napa
Phone: (707) 255-7700
Hours: 10-4 weekdays
Winemaker: John Trefethen, David Whitehouse
Facilities: retail sales
Wines: varietal
Vineyards: 500 acres
Volume: 106,500 fermenting, 10,000 cases annually

VEEDERCREST VINEYARDS—Page 177
Address: Mt. Veeder Rd. at Lokoya Rd., Napa; mailing
address: 1401 Standord Ave., Emeryville
Phone: (415) 652-3103
Hours: not open to public
Facilities: tours by appointment
Winemaker: Alfred W. Baxter
Wines: varietals
Volume: 8,500 cases

VILLA MT. EDEN—Page 91
Address: P.O. Box 147, Oakville
Phone: (707) 944-8431
Hours: phone for appointment
Facilities: arranged by appointment
Winemaker: Nils Venge
Wines: varietals
Vineyards: 87 acres
Volume: 10,000 gallons fermenting, 4,000 cases annually

YVERDON VINEYARDS—Page 135
Address: 3728 Spring Mountain Road, St. Helena
Phone: (707) 963-3266
Hours: not open to public
Facilities: none available
Winemaker: Fred Aves
Wines: varietals
Vineyards: 110 acres
Volume: 50,000 gallons storage; 25,000 gallons fermenting